Cambridge Elements ≡

Elements on Women in the History of Philosophy
edited by
Jacqueline Broad
Monash University

EARLY CHRISTIAN WOMEN

Dawn LaValle Norman
Australian Catholic University

CAMBRIDGE
UNIVERSITY PRESS

CAMBRIDGE
UNIVERSITY PRESS

University Printing House, Cambridge CB2 8BS, United Kingdom

One Liberty Plaza, 20th Floor, New York, NY 10006, USA

477 Williamstown Road, Port Melbourne, VIC 3207, Australia

314–321, 3rd Floor, Plot 3, Splendor Forum, Jasola District Centre,
New Delhi – 110025, India

103 Penang Road, #05–06/07, Visioncrest Commercial, Singapore 238467

Cambridge University Press is part of the University of Cambridge.

It furthers the University's mission by disseminating knowledge in the pursuit of
education, learning, and research at the highest international levels of excellence.

www.cambridge.org
Information on this title: www.cambridge.org/9781009045889
DOI: 10.1017/9781009047067

First published 2022

A catalogue record for this publication is available from the British Library.

ISBN 978-1-009-04588-9 Paperback
ISSN 2634-4645 (online)
ISSN 2634-4637 (print)

Early Christian Women

Elements on Women in the History of Philosophy

DOI: 10.1017/9781009047067
First published online: August 2022

Dawn LaValle Norman
Australian Catholic University

Author for correspondence: Dawn LaValle Norman, dawn.lavallenorman@acu.edu.au

Abstract: In this Element, the author argues that genre deeply affects how early Christian female philosophers are characterized across different works. The included case studies are three women who feature in both narrative and dialogic texts: Thecla, Macrina the Younger, and Monica. Based on these examples, the author demonstrates that the narrative sources tend to eschew secular education, while the dialogic sources are open to displays of secular knowledge. Philosophy was seen not only as a way of life but sometimes also as a mode of educated argumentation. The author further argues that these female philosophers were held up in their femininity as models for imitation by both women and men.

Keywords: ancient female philosophers, early Christian women, Thecla, Macrina, Monica

ISBNs: 9781009045889 (PB), 9781009047067 (OC)
ISSNs: 2634-4645 (online), 2634-4637 (print)

Contents

1 Introduction: Lady Philosophy and Real Female Philosophers

Women were prizes men competed for in the ancient world, both in life and in literature. Greco-Roman writers constructed a tradition that cast the goal of the good life as a desirable woman. Prodicus' "Choice of Heracles" (Xenophon *Memorabilia* 2.1) narrates an allegorical encounter between Heracles and two women: Virtue (*Arete*) and Vice (*Kakia*). The anonymous *Tabula of Cebes* imagines Happiness (*Eudaimonia*) surrounded by her daughters the Virtues as the true goal of education, in contrast with false learning (*Tabula of Cebes* II.20). Lucian's *The Teacher of Rhetoric* presents two contrasting routes up the mountain to join Lady Rhetoric.[1] This tradition was to flower in Boethius' sixth-century encounter with Lady Philosophy in the *Consolation of Philosophy*, a gendered allegorization that echoed down through the ages (Courcelle 1970; Helleman 2009; Tervahauta et al. 2017).

The personification of philosophy as a woman assumes that philosophers, her erotic desirers, are symbolically masculine. The binary of male lover–female beloved imagines that the target of such pleas are men who were inspired by the idea of choosing wisely between competing types of women. Yet in the third century CE, the Christian dialogue writer Methodius of Olympus reimagined the gendered relationships of allegorical females in educational ascent myths. Virtue, daughter of Philosophy, still dwelt on top of a mountain that was steep and dangerous. But instead of questing men who attempted to enter her secluded garden, educated women were invited to her garden party (LaValle Norman 2019b, 188–92).

Simultaneously, other Christian groups were writing narratives about a fall of Sophia (Wisdom) into the world of the material. The story of her return through the dangers posed at different levels of her cosmic ascent inspired Christians in their own struggles.[2] Wisdom herself in such narratives is required to return up the mountain, with humans invited to join imaginatively in Wisdom's salvific drama. In such narratives, the journey itself is feminized, and humans are united with the female Wisdom figure in her ascent rather than the female Wisdom being placed as the goal of that ascent.

In addition to the erotic pursuit of a feminized Wisdom, there were deeper connections between the life of virtue and manliness in the ancient world, many of them recurrent and etymological. The Latin word for virtue, *virtus*, stems from the word for man, *vir*, as does the Greek word for courage, *andreia/*

---

[1] Douglas Whalin has recently written on the role of the mountain of ascent in such narratives (Whalin 2021).

[2] "Sophia's act of hybris and subsequent fall lie at the very heart of the Gnostic's understanding of his own existential predicament" (Goehring 1981, 16).

ἀνδρεία (anēr/ἀνήρ = man). The etymological links assured the perennial connection between virtue, courage, and manliness in the ancient world (Rosen and Sluiter 2003). As a result, many studies have focused on how female philosophers and holy women "become male" to achieve the ideal life (e.g. Miles 1989; Castelli 1991; Cloke 1994; Aspegren 1995). I would like to look at another side of the story, at those moments when women were permitted to be models of the philosophical life in their femininity, inviting their auditors and readers to "become female" in a certain sense.

If women were allowed to become philosophical models *in their femininity*, could the life of philosophy continue to be one thing? Or were there different expectations for what a "female philosopher" would look like instead of a "male philosopher"? Or does gender have nothing to do with it at all and is just a distraction from the real issues of philosophy and the good life?

A helpful instantiation of some of the complexities around this set of questions can be found in Clement of Alexandria's introduction to his book on correct Christian behavior, the *Paedagogus*. Clement, writing in the second century CE, insists on the equality of women and men in the Christian life, and even the eschatological unimportance of gender, building on Paul's assertion in Galatians 3:38. Yet, he also admits that "in this world" gender shapes almost every aspect of experience:[3]

> for this world is the only place in which the female is distinguished from the male, "but in that other world, no longer." There, the rewards of this life, lived in the holy union of wedlock, await not man or woman as such, but the human person, freed from the lust that in this life had made them either male or female. (Clement of Alexandria *Paedagogus* 1.4.10, trans. Wood pp. 11–12)
>
> ἐν ᾧ δὴ μόνῳ τὸ θῆλυ τοῦ ἄρρενος διακρίνεται, "ἐν ἐκείνῳ δὲ οὐκέτι," ἔνθα τοῦ κοινωνικοῦ καὶ ἁγίου τούτου βίου τοῦ ἐκ συζυγίας τὰ ἔπαθλα οὐκ ἄρρενι καὶ θηλείᾳ, ἀνθρώπῳ δὲ ἀπόκειται ἐπιθυμίας διχαζούσης αὐτὸν κεχωρισμένῳ.

Clement asserts the ideological unity of humanity, beyond gender. Yet at the same time, he admits that "in this world" gender persists. In line with this understanding, the content of his advice in the rest of the book is frequently gender-specific and draws repeatedly on social attitudes about appropriate deportment rather than theological concepts (Leyerle 1995).

In this Element, I will investigate the tension between the Christian belief in a unity of humanity beyond gender and gender-specific expectations of a philosophical life. Is there a way that women were believed to "do"

---

[3] For an outline of some lines of interpretation of Galatians 3:38, see chapter 6, "Neither Male Nor Female" in Fiorenza 1994, 205–41.

philosophy distinct from how men did it? And if so, then why were men interested in portraying them as philosophers? I will look at three examples of early Christian women who are presented as models of ideal philosophers and analyze them in chronological order. We do not have any texts written by these three women, nor, in fact, do their biographers claim that they wrote any. Like Socrates, their teaching is purely oral. As a result, men moderate our access to these women and their philosophy, and, in two of the three instances, the women are intimately connected through family ties with the male authors who depict them, as sister and mother respectively.

Thecla, whose story was written earliest, started as a companion of St. Paul before she began her own journey as an itinerant teacher. Works about her abound from the second to the fifth centuries, but it was especially in Methodius of Olympus' *Symposium* (c. 290 CE) where she was presented and characterized as a philosopher surrounded by other philosophical women. My second example, Macrina the Younger, was memorialized as a philosopher and teacher in two texts written by her brother Gregory of Nyssa in the mid-fourth century, one a biography and one a philosophical dialogue. Finally, Augustine's mother Monica is written as an active participant in Augustine's Cassiciacum dialogues, where Augustine praises her excellent grasp of philosophy, in addition to the influential role in his life he ascribes to her in his autobiographical *Confessions*.

Each of these three women is presented as wise across genres. In their biographies, the issue of the relationship between gender and wisdom is narrated and displayed by drawing upon tropes and exempla from previous traditions. The authors reveal how the holiness of these women's lives, rather than their academic accomplishments, gives them direct access to wisdom. The content of their wisdom is not discursively shown but rather implied. In philosophical dialogues, on the other hand, the reader reads what men imagine women to be capable of thinking and saying. Dialogues focus on the speech of wise women rather than their actions, showing a particular type of knowledge through dialectic and verbal display. In each of the three examples I will look at, the biographical texts do not reproduce the women in verbal mode at length. This in and of itself is interesting, since there were well-established ways to embed the verbal philosopher into narrative texts. To name two from either side of the religious divide of late antiquity, Philostratus' *Life of Apollonius of Tyana* and Athanasius' *Life of Anthony* both reproduce and not just report debates between their subjects and other philosophers. Yet, the writer of the *Acts of Paul and Thecla*, Gregory of Nyssa, and Augustine do not include lengthy speeches of the women in their biographical texts. They separate the example of the philosophical lives lived by these women from their verbal engagement with ideas.

But they style them as philosophers in both. The life of philosophy can be wielded in different contexts with a range of associations.

I have intentionally chosen examples of women in early Christianity who are not only described as living philosophically but also shown speaking philosophically. Within the philosophical tradition, there was a long-standing definition of philosophy that focused on the way that a philosopher lived, rather than on their discursive knowledge or verbal agility. The moral emphasis intensified in Christianity, where many writers delighted in showing people who led a "philosophical life," by which they meant an ascetical life that resulted in correctly ordered desires, often coupled with a lack of formal education.

Pierre Hadot made famous this idea, popularizing the concept that ancient philosophy was "a way of life." He meant by this that all the different philosophical sects shared the conviction that to pursue wisdom was to learn to see reality correctly and then to live according to that vision (Hadot 1995, 58). Chief among the witnesses to one's correct vision of reality was the ability to approach death well (Hadot 1995, 59). Such a vision- and practice-oriented view of philosophy could embrace a range of uneducated individuals, and many hagiographical texts tapped into this broader understanding of the philosophical life. Relationships between teachers and students were not of primary importance in such narratives, where the philosopher in question might have access to wisdom through alternative channels such as direct divine inspiration. Anne-Marie Malingrey has provided corroborating evidence of this thesis by collating the changing valences of the "philosophy" word group from antiquity into early Christianity, revealing just how varied the interpretations could be. What persisted, she argues, is the idea of philosophy as the "intelligence moved by love" (Malingrey 1961, 290), which functions under different modalities through time.

But there was a narrower understanding of philosophy active in this period, which can be labeled "professional philosophy" (Dillon 2004), namely the life of teachers and students working within philosophical traditions. Such educational networks were certainly concerned with the ethical life, like the broader group of "philosophers," but approached it via a course of study that typically involved reading certain texts and coming to understand specific doctrines. Iamblichus' Neopythagorean course of study is an excellent example of this (O'Meara 1990, 33–34). This narrower definition of the "philosophical life" will be a primary lens through which I look at the three women covered in this Element.[4] I will pursue questions surrounding narratives about the education of

---

[4] Other scholars have pursued this question for different ancient philosophical traditions, e.g. Pythagoreanism (Dutsch 2020; Pellò 2022), the Platonic Academy (Dorandi 1989; Addey 2017), and the Aristotelian tradition (Deslauriers 2022; Connell 2016).

women and their verbal display of textual knowledge. This type of philosophy is more important to writers when they script their women into dialogues, where actions are often missing entirely, or underplayed, and the philosophical status of the speaker must instead be shown through educated discourse.

Marguerite Deslauriers has laid down the gauntlet about this narrower type of philosophy and its relationship to women in the ancient world.

> Philosophy, then as now, was a social practice, engagement with which was predicated on education and on certain social freedoms, neither of which women enjoyed. (Deslauriers 2012, 345)

I would like to challenge this stark view, suggesting that room was made for a certain amount of social philosophical life for women in the ancient world. My three examples all present different versions of this social philosophical life and, in particular, different relationships between the genders of the teacher–student relationships. The *Acts of Paul and Thecla* and Methodius' *Symposium* present Thecla solely as a teacher of other women; *On the Soul and Resurrection* presents Macrina as a female teacher of her male brother; Augustine's Cassiciacum dialogues paradoxically present Monica as the female student of her male child. Female–female teaching circles, female–male and male–female educative modes all find expression. All configurations are covered, the homo-social as well as the heterosocial, the familial and the pseudofamilial.

In terms of the relationship between the literary depictions of social philo-sophical life and history, my analysis in this Element broadly follows in the tradition of Elizabeth Clark's work on the "Macrina-function" and "Monica-function" in those writings of Gregory of Nyssa and Augustine that are also analyzed in this Element (E. A. Clark 1998; E. Clark 1999). I agree with Clark that the question that is most interesting, and most answerable, when analyzing women in these texts is how they are being wielded in male-centric debates, whether philosophical or theological. However, I think that Clark missed out an important, even fundamental, element in her analysis of Macrina in Gregory of Nyssa's work: genre. Clark underdescribes the *Life of Macrina* and *On the Soul and Resurrection* as "two treatises that focus on his sister Macrina."[5] Much work on Macrina has done the same, tying together her depictions in the two works by Gregory of Nyssa (Krueger 2000; Frank 2000; J. W. Smith 2004; Champion 2014). I believe that paying attention to the difference in how women are used when they are in dialogic mode rather than biographical mode can

---

[5] She is more careful to distinguish the Cassiciacum dialogues from the *Confessions* in her companion piece on the "Monica-function" in Augustine's work but still does not investigate the problem of genre, instead speaking about the different theological purposes of the works (E. Clark 1999, 15).

bring us closer to the heart of the question of what it meant to be depicted as a female philosopher in Christian writing during the first four centuries.

Do these literary depictions, or "women-functions," in a text have anything to do with historical female philosophers? A helpful intervention was made by Virginia Burrus, when talking about "strategically" attempting to get behind male texts portraying verbal women to "historical" women (as a presumed nod to the "strategic essentialism" of Gayatri Spivak).

> What I am getting at is the possibility that the discursive space occupied earlier by Plato's Diotima and flute girl, or here by Gregory's Macrina, might also correlate, however inexactly, with the social roles and influence of women: that the textual production of an articulable feminine positionality via the interaction of the female as "object" and the female as the excluded transgressive, may at least indirectly point toward actual subject positions and social roles available to and occupiable by women historically "as women." The representations of women in male-centered texts may stand in for, without exactly reproducing, the intrusive presence of women in the always incomplete formation of male homosocial communities. (Burrus 2005, 259)

Another way of saying this is that, despite being constrained by the always-constructed literary representations that are (by and large) our only witnesses to these women, bounded by genre and a range of theological intentions of their authors, nevertheless there are some connections between the philosophical lives of early Christian women and the discourse around such women that will form the heart of my analysis. Elizabeth Clark herself, in her treatment of the Monica-function, admits that we are still left with "traces" of Monica, textualized and historicized (E. Clark 1999, 21). Methodius, Gregory, and Augustine were presenting their written women within the realm of the possible for their readers.

In addition, their stories both reflect and enact change. Gregory says in his biography of Macrina that their mother had a dream where an angel called her unborn child Thecla. Gregory says that this was to foretell that Macrina and Thecla would share the same choices in life (τὴν τῆς προαιρέσεως ὁμοιότητα, Greg. Nyss. *Vit. Macr.* 3.3 Silvas/2 Maraval). Thecla's "choices" were real to Macrina's mother, at least according to Gregory. Thecla's story acts in later generations even if Thecla never existed as a person. The turn to "reception studies" is one way of getting beyond the difficult relationship between the literary portrayal of female roles and the historical reality of women (Davis 2015).

I argue two related theses in this Element, with different vibrancies for each of the three examples, and will treat both theses at the conclusion of each section. First, I argue that an important impetus for women being described as philosophers in this period was a change in the definition of philosophy that no longer required education along traditional channels. This was a complicated process, and each author came up with a different version of the balance of value. A liberal arts education was valuable enough for Methodius to invent one for Thecla. Yet it was not important for Augustine's version of Monica's philosophy, which had its source elsewhere.

Second, many studies have focused on how female philosophers and holy women "become male" to achieve the ideal life, a point I have already touched upon. I will argue an alternative story in this Element that male readers of these texts are invited to "become female" in their imaginations, to take on some of the characteristics traditionally gendered feminine in the ancient world, which have been reimagined as acceptable parts of the virtuous man and ideal citizen.[6] This is a true revolution, even if it has more to do with male constructions of the female than with women themselves.

Other Elements in this series, Women in the History of Philosophy, especially Crystal Addey's *Platonist and Neoplatonist Women*, cover women living in the same centuries as those covered in this one and even some, like Hypatia of Alexandria, who lived after all of the three women I will analyze. Strong bonds connect such philosophical women across religious conviction: the fact that this Element covers only Christian women is not meant to argue that they belong to a separate genealogy from women such as Porphyry's wife Marcella or the mystical philosopher Sosipatra.[7] Nevertheless, Christianity provided some distinct scripts for female philosophers, reflecting and building community expectations about what was possible. And these distinct scripts were constrained by the expectations of the genre, whether narrative or dialogic.

2 Thecla, "Second to None in Philosophy and the Liberal Arts" (Meth. *Symp.* 8.170)

Thecla did not start her literary life as a philosopher, but she became one as her legend developed. While her philosopher status was something that was only added later in the tradition, she was honored from her entrance onto the literary stage in the *Acts of Paul and Thecla* as a teacher. In this section, I will analyze how her teaching career is depicted in this hagiographical work, before turning to the way in which her story was taken up and modified in the following century by moving her into a philosophical dialogue.

---

[6] Ellen Muehlberger and I have made such arguments in two recent articles (Muehlberger 2015; LaValle Norman 2019a). This is a different argument to that propounded by Kate Cooper, who argues that ancient narratives of female ascetics are not about female liberation but about male concerns. Cooper does not push this argument to suggest that the women in these stories might be objects of identification for their male readers (Cooper 1996).

[7] For example, it has been recently argued that Eunapius' characterization of Sosipatra is a direct response to the rise of female intellectual saints in Christianity (Marx 2021, 14).

Thecla is characterized as a disciple and evangelist in the *Acts of Paul and Thecla*, fitting under the rubric of "wandering charismatic" (Davis 2008, 26–35). Just as strongly, as I will argue, she is characterized as a daughter, both biologically and allegorically. Although she is not characterized as a philosopher, there were enough clues in this direction to allow Methodius of Olympus approximately one hundred years later to develop her characterization from preacher and teacher to philosopher. And Thecla's feminine characterization made both moves surprising in parallel ways. The surprise of the female wandering teacher paved the way for the surprise of the female philosopher to emerge in a different setting.

Thecla is unique among my examples not only because I will trace her character's development across two different authors' representations but also because most scholars agree that she was not a historical person. While my inclinations always lean toward inclusivity where proof of nonexistence is impossible,[8] the historicity of Thecla does not affect the argument that I will make here. Thecla became a model of the female philosopher in the development of her story over time, both in Methodius of Olympus' *Symposium* and in Gregory of Nyssa's *Life of Macrina*.

The treatment of Thecla first as an itinerant teacher and then as a philosopher in the *Acts of Paul and Thecla* and Methodius' *Symposium* sets the groundwork for how the dynamic of female philosophical characterization plays out in the narrative and dialogic texts written by Gregory of Nyssa and Augustine. The narrative texts consistently resist giving philosophical speeches to wise females, who instead display their philosophy through actions, especially their relationship to the prospect of death, rather than words. Only when the characters are inserted into dialogues do they take on discursive functions that often show evidence, or make claims, of a formal philosophical education, or need to be explicit in their rejection of that claim, as in the case of Monica.

2.1 The *Acts of Paul and Thecla*

The *Acts of Paul and Thecla* portrays Thecla's growth from new convert to teacher.[9] But for a story arc focused on the assumption of teaching duties, there is precious little in the text about the content of the teaching that Thecla dedicates her life to preaching. In fact, rather than focusing on listening and speaking, which would seem to be the normal mode of education, the focus of the *Acts of Paul and Thecla*

---

[8] "It is conceivable that behind the tradition of Thecla lies a historical woman, who ultimately came to be linked with the figure of Paul, but we have no way to determine this" (Kraemer 1992, 154).

[9] For all of the citations of the *Acts of Paul and Thecla*, I will use the numeration of Jeremy Barrier (Barrier 2009).

remains decidedly on seeing and being visible.[10] This goes hand in hand with the author's primary concern to prove Thecla's status through her displays of endurance rather than verbally evidenced wisdom.

The *Acts of Paul and Thecla* is the earliest witness to the story of Thecla as a disciple of Paul. It was most likely written between 150 and 200 CE, and Tertullian's condemnation of Thecla's self-baptism in *De Baptismo* 17 provides the widely accepted *terminus ante quem* (Rordorf 1986).[11] Dennis MacDonald has influentially argued that the oral legends behind the *Acts of Paul and Thecla* originated in circles of ascetic female Christians in Asia Minor, citing the sympathy toward female characters (human and animal) and negativity toward male characters as evidence (MacDonald 1983, 34–37). While I am not as convinced as MacDonald that a pro-woman text is most likely to be *composed* by a woman, imagining the *reception* of this work in female circles is a natural response to the content of a work so focused on female sociality (Kraemer 2019: 498–499).

Tertullian, when he comes to condemn the *Acts of Paul*, points to two things in particular that are egregious in the text: female teaching and baptizing.

> Certain Acts of Paul, which are falsely so named, claim the example of Thecla for allowing women to teach and to baptize (*docendi tinguendique*) ... How could we believe that Paul should give a female power to teach and to baptize (*docendi et tinguendi*), when he did not allow a woman even to learn by her own right? Let them keep silence, he says, and ask their husbands at home.
> (Tertullian *de baptismo* 17, trans. Evans 1964, 37)

> quae Acta Pauli, quae perperam scripta sunt, exemplum Theclae ad licentiam mulierum docendi tinguendique defendant ... quam enim fidei proximum videtur ut is docendi et tinguendi daret feminae potestatem qui ne discere quidem constanter mulieri permisit? Taceant, inquit, et domi viros suos consulant.

Tertullian makes an a fortiori argument: if Paul did not allow women to *learn* in public (1 Corinthians 14:34) then certainly he would not allow them to *teach*. Familial questioning was an option but nothing that brought that

---

[10] While concerned with the same nexus of issues, my argument is in direct contradiction to the conclusion of Jennifer Eyl: "The net result of this excision [of erōs], for our author, is a privileging of the voice and ears over the appearance and eyes" (Eyl 2013, 15).

[11] Although I note the objection of Stevan L. Davies to the identification of Tertullian's Thecla source with the *Acts of Paul and Thecla* (Davies 1986). There is debate about the relationship between the *Acts of Paul and Thecla* and the longer *Acts of Paul* which contain it. Most scholars think that the *Acts of Paul and Thecla* is the older material that is absorbed into the *Acts of Paul*, especially those who emphasize the orality behind the legends of the *Acts of Paul and Thecla* (MacDonald 1983). For our purposes, we can leave aside the larger *Acts of Paul* to focus only on the *Acts of Paul and Thecla*, which had a separate transmission history and a separate editing process in the modern period.

questioning into public, thereby necessitating a relationship with an external teacher.[12] Since Tertullian's criticism of Thecla is her public preaching, it is all the more surprising that the text under fire included so little of the *content* of that teaching. Neither is it straightforwardly concerned with outlining a Pauline succession: Thecla does not begin a line of teachers (D. E. Smith 2002, 112).

2.1.1 Thecla as Student in the Acts of Paul and Thecla

A question we must address is whether Thecla's assumption of teaching authority is aligned with the life of philosophy. Leslie Hayes argues that the portrayal of Paul in this story shifts from wonder-worker to philosopher when the narrative enters the *Acts of Paul and Thecla* from the surrounding *Acts of Paul* material. When it does so, Thecla takes over the wonder-working abilities from Paul's character in the story. The author of the Thecla material makes this intentional move, Hayes argues, in order to focus on succession itself rather than on teaching content: authority structures interest the author of the text more than the content of the teaching (Hayes 2016, 25–26, 208). I agree that the focus of the *Acts of Paul and Thecla* is on authority. But one difficulty with Hayes' suggestion is that Thecla does not in turn hand on the teaching to others at the end of her life but rather becomes a stable geographical source of inspiration at her shrine, even after her death. If the story is about succession, it is only about one link in a succession chain. A second difficulty is that the *Acts of Paul and Thecla* never uses the words philosophy, philosopher, or philosophize, either for Thecla or for Paul.

As scholars such as Stevan L. Davies, Dennis MacDonald, Virginia Burrus, and Ross Shepard Kraemer, among others, have emphasized, female power structures are important in this text (Davies 1980; MacDonald 1983; Davies 1986; Burrus 1987; Kraemer 1992 and 2019). While Thecla pursues Paul in order to gain the bestowal of teaching authority, her desire is continually frustrated. Instead, the text shifts the focus onto multiple mother–daughter relationships and their concomitant social responsibilities.

Thecla's entrance into the *Acts of Paul and Thecla* is situated within the social bonds of family, and her family structure is emphatically feminine. She is described as "Thecla, the virgin daughter of her mother Theocleia" (Θέκλα τις παρθένος Θεοκλείας μητρός, *ATh* 3.7). She is only given a matronymic. Since her father is not mentioned in the entire text one is left to presume that he is

---

[12] Domestic philosophical education, however, was a well-respected avenue for female philosophers (G. Clark 2007).

dead.[13] The link is so tight between Thecla and her mother, Theocleia, that their names differ only by the addition of four letters in the Greek. Thecla's maternal connections are further emphasized as the narrative progresses and she takes on a new adoptive mother in Queen Tryphaena (*ATh* 4.3). Additionally, at the end of the narrative, she returns to her mother, begging her to join her way of life, even offering her material wealth to make up for what she had lost through her daughter. Rather than a father, the man mentioned in Thecla's initial identifying sentence is her betrothed, Thamyris. Yet when Thecla returns to her hometown of Iconium, Thamyris has died (*ATh* 4.18), just as Paul has also dropped out of the narrative. The mother figures persist even after the lover figures have been replaced with a divine spouse.

At her introduction into the text, Thecla is not only placed into a mother–daughter social structure that will persist throughout the text but is also given a complicated relationship to seeing and hearing. She is sitting indoors, where she belongs, but also next to a window, which provides a point of access to the outside world. A window would seem to be primarily about seeing – after all, one can hear through walls.[14] Yet Thecla does not use the window to see but rather to hear a speech about chastity that Paul has been giving (ἤκουεν νυκτὸς καὶ ἡμέρας τὸν περὶ ἁγνείας λόγον λεγόμενον ὑπὸ τοῦ Παύλου, *ATh* 3.7). There are in fact two walls between Thecla and Paul, who is likewise sitting inside. Sound alone forms the initial attraction.[15] But the sound creates a desire to *see* Paul, which drives the narrative of much of the rest of the text.

> But yet seeing many women and virgins going in to Paul, she herself desired to be made worthy to stand in the presence of Paul and to hear the word of Christ, for she had not yet seen the characteristics of Paul, but was only hearing his speech. (Barrier 2009, 86)

---

[13] This is a very rare way of identifying someone in documentary papyri. For instance, in only 10 percent of the instances of matronymics analyzed by Broux and Depauw is the matronymic used by itself. More normally, a matronymic, if included, is combined with a patronymic (Broux and Depauw 2015, 472). Importantly, one common literary place where exclusive matronymics are used is in contexts of the "families" of prostitutes, for instance, in Lucian's *Dialogues of the Prostitutes*. This implies that such matronymics are more common in female professions – there are simply very few of these.

[14] Eyl calls the window "a nearly overdetermined metaphor for visual perception," arguing that the author places her there to raise the reader's awareness that they are disrupting the novelistic template of love at first *sight* (Eyl 2013, 11–12). Eyl is right that the author is playing with novelistic tropes, but she fails to account for Thecla's continued desire to see Paul.

[15] Nevertheless, Thecla *has* been looking out the window and seeing something – the other women of Iconium who are coming and going from Onesiphorus' house to hear the teaching of Paul in person. The women of the city, who are supposed to be inside, are the ones who are visible to Thecla's gaze, coming and going on the street, visiting a sequestered Paul. The passage where we first meet Thecla is full of inversions of gendered expectations of inside-outside and the politics of sight.

ἔτι δὲ καὶ **βλέπουσα** πολλὰς γυναῖκας καὶ παρθένους εἰσπορευομένας πρὸς τὸν Παῦλον, ἐπεπόθει καὶ αὐτὴ καταξιωθῆναι **κατὰ πρόσωπον στῆναι Παύλου καὶ ἀκούειν** τὸν τοῦ Χριστοῦ λόγον· οὐδέπω γὰρ τὸν χαρακτῆρα Παύλου **ἑωράκει**, ἀλλὰ τοῦ λόγου **ἤκουεν** μόνον.

Thecla says that she has not yet seen but only heard Paul. She subordinates hearing to seeing, which is a hoped-for future event. But why, if Thecla wants to become a student of Paul, does she need to see him at all? Surely hearing his teaching would be sufficient. But no, there is a marked emphasis on vision throughout this text. The depiction of Thecla's discipleship in the *Acts of Paul and Thecla* revolves around the sense of vision.[16] Thecla tries to watch, succeeds in watching, and finally is watched by multiple crowds, before ultimately being seen by Paul and granted her teaching authority. I argue that the emphasis on vision in the text goes hand in hand with the absence of teaching content in the narratives about Thecla's status, to which I will turn next.

2.1.2 Thecla as Teacher in the Acts of Paul and Thecla

Thecla can only become a true student of Paul once she sees him – hearing is not sufficient. She leaves her house and joins him in prison (*ATh* 3.18). On the next day, both Paul and Thecla are brought before the governor (*ATh* 3.19). Just as when she was at the window of her own house, she is completely oriented toward Paul and is silent when spoken to by anyone else. But her desire to see Paul has finally been satisfied. The word used for her gazing attention, ἀτενίζω, is used across key points in the *Acts of Paul and Thecla* (*ATh* 3.8, 3.9, 3.20, 3.21). It is only once Paul and Thecla are separated, and Thecla alone sentenced to death, that the language of sight reaches its height (*ATh* 3.21). She earnestly searches for Paul like a lamb looking for her shepherd, thinks she sees him (it is really Christ), says that he is gazing on her in a moment of wonderful mutuality, only to have him disappear again (*ATh* 3.21). Entirely suitably, the moment of heightened seeing takes place in a theater – the ancient location etymologically associated with seeing. In fact, the author makes this pun themselves: Thecla is taken into the theater (*thea-tron*), where a crowd comes to see the spectacle (*theorias*) (εἰς τὸν **θέατρον**. Καὶ πᾶς ὁ ὄχλος ἐξῆλθεν ἐπὶ τὴν ἀνάγκην τῆς **θεωρίας**, *ATh* 3.21).

---

[16] Eyl has examined the overturning of sensory tropes from the novel in the *Acts of Paul and Thecla*. While she rightly concludes that the author of the *Acts* is intentionally avoiding allowing Thecla and Paul to look at each other, I do not think that Eyl appreciates the entirety of the impact of the shift. Yes, it is partly to do with the avoidance of eros, but not entirely (Eyl 2013).

Thus begins the first scene of trials that are literally theatrical in Thecla's home town of Iconium. But Thecla's story continues in another city, Antioch, with another set of public spectacles. There, Paul as the one gazed upon and gazing back (or is it Christ?) is removed. Instead, it is Thecla alone who becomes the spectacle. She fights wild beasts unharmed, self-baptizes in a pool of deadly seals (who are immediately killed with lightning), and comes through an attempt to have her torn apart by bulls unscathed. The reactions of the spectators are recorded, with the women of the city consistently on her side. Only after all of this is she taken away from the theater and brought before the governor. In the equivalent scene a bit earlier, the governor asked Paul what it was that he was *teaching*, and he responded with a speech full of theological content, relating the basic outline of his Christian commitments (*ATh* 3.17). Thecla, on the other hand, is not asked what it is that she has been teaching, because she has not yet been certified and her teaching career lies ahead of her. Instead, the governor asks her why the beasts do not touch her (*ATh* 4.12). The text focuses on her endurance rather than her teaching. Thecla is at her most persuasive when she is on visual display, both to those internal to the text and to the readers of the *Acts*. Her short reply at this moment is given particular power because of the spectacle she has just presented.

The power of Thecla's spectacle is enough to "evangelize" a rich woman of Antioch named Tryphaena (καὶ τὴν Τρύφαιναν εὐαγγελισθεῖσαν, *ATh* 4.14). Thecla's endurance rather than her preaching leads Tryphaena to her expression of faith ("Now I believe [πιστεύω] that the dead are raised. Now I believe [πιστεύω] that my child lives," *ATh* 4.14). Tryphaena welcomes Thecla into her house, and finally Thecla is said to preach, using the verb κατηχέω, which is the one favored in the New Testament for preaching (e.g. 1 Corinthians 14:19; Galatians 6:6; Luke 1:4; Acts 18:12). As a result of her preaching, Tryphaena "believed in God" (ὥστε πιστεῦσαι τῷ θεῷ, *ATh* 4.14). The author doubles Tryphaena's "belief" in the resurrection of the dead that she pronounced as a result of Thecla's spectacle with a "belief" in God as a result of Thecla's preaching. Thecla becomes Tryphaena's heir, explicitly replacing her deceased daughter Falconilla, and Tryphaena's whole household is converted through the influential female head (*ATh* 4.13). Thecla's teaching here is modeled on the Scriptures more than a philosophical succession. And the relationship that is most emphasized is between mother and daughter.

After Thecla has survived her trials and left Antioch, she journeys to visit Paul in Myra. To mark her transition, she makes and dons new clothes – specifically a *chiton* (*ATh* 4.15). Unlike Justin Martyr (*Dialogue with Trypho* 1.2), she does not don the *tribon*, the philosopher's outer cloak, but a full-length garment that was used by both men and women, although Thecla is said to wear it in a masculine fashion (σχήατι ἀνδρικῶι).[17] I argue that, despite wearing a chiton in a "masculine way," her preaching role is still done in a "feminine way" and even a distinctly filial way.

At this point, Paul finally confirms Thecla as a teacher: "Go and teach the word of God" (Ὕπαγε καὶ δίδασκε τὸν λόγον τοῦ θεοῦ, *ATh* 4.16). In response to this command, Thecla makes the unexpected choice to return home to Iconium and, once arrived, enter the house next to hers whence she heard Paul teach when she listened from her window. She falls to the ground where Paul had sat and taught her the oracles of God. Thecla now can enter the house symbolically for the first time, joining herself to her desired goal from the beginning of her drama (Barrier 2009, 186). Hearing has never been enough for this narrative that is focused on the spectacular assumption of charismatic power.

Inside the empty house of Onesiphorus, Thecla gives one of her only lengthy speeches, a prayer which she "cries out" (*ATh* 4.17). This is one of Thecla's most theologically rich utterances in the *Acts*, a rhythmically repeating prayer of thanksgiving for deliverance from her many trials. Conducted in private, its function is not to teach but rather to praise. The focus is on the events of her life as witnesses of God's mercy rather than the theological or philosophical content of her faith.

In this house that holds the memory of Paul's physical and visual presence, Thecla performs the only witnessing recorded after she has been given the teaching mandate by Paul. She summons her mother to her, who is presumably still living in the house next door. She tells her mother that she will have her daughter and her riches restored to her (from the money given to her by her adoptive mother Tryphaena), if only she becomes a Christian. Having performed this witness (καὶ ταῦτα διαμαρτυραμένη, *ATh* 4.18), Thecla leaves. Her conversation with her mother is not spoken of in terms of teaching or philosophizing but of witnessing. The content of the witness is the offer to fulfill the debt that she incurred upon leaving. Her speech and actions fill the role of a daughter rather than being scripted for a philosopher.

Unlike other *Acts*, Thecla does not give lengthy speeches of exhortation or teaching. She only briefly slips into verbal mode. Instead, her teaching is demonstrated by her constancy in the face of trials and later in her ascetic way of life, rather than in words. It is in this mode that she is at her most powerful and able to persuade through the sense of vision alone, even without content-rich speech.

---

[17] For scholarship on early Christian cross-dressing, including Thecla's, see the work of Valerie Hotchkiss (Hotchkiss 1996, 20–21), Stephen Davis (Davis 2002), and Kristi Upson-Saia (Upson-Saia 2011, 84–103).

2.1.3 Conclusion

The *Acts of Paul and Thecla* dramatizes Thecla's transition from student to teacher through her frustrated desire to *see*. Hand in hand with the focus on sight over hearing, the content of Thecla's teaching is limited. Her conversion is not specifically styled as a philosophical conversion: rather than a philosopher, she is a spectacle and she is a daughter. There are some important moments of masculinization of Thecla in the narrative. She wears a chiton "in a masculine fashion," and she offers to cut her hair short. Nevertheless, Thecla remains strongly gendered feminine in her consistent identification as daughter. Despite trying in the whole work to be a follower of Paul, it is female relationships that prove to be the most important in this text.

Thecla follows Paul and becomes his disciple without any evidence or need for a traditional education. Instead of the long and slow process of education, she endures a different (and more painful) process of certification. It takes her suffering in the arena to raise herself to a legitimate level to prove to Paul that she can take on a teaching mandate. Thecla's speech in the arena is only made possible after her heroic endurance tests. And her longest speech takes place when she is entirely alone in Onesiphorus' house. The *Acts of Paul and Thecla* locates Thecla's witness in her endurance rather than education. The focus on suffering and endurance will continue in the next text where she features as a character, but it will be augmented with a traditional liberal arts education as well.

2.2 Thecla the Philosopher in Methodius of Olympus' *Symposium*

When Thecla moves from the *Acts* into a philosophical dialogue, her characterization changes. She is still the valiant woman who withstands the attacks of the wild beasts and is a direct disciple of Paul. But she is also explicitly called a philosopher and functions in the presence of a group of female philosophers. But while she moves from being a charismatic (albeit content-light) teacher to being a philosopher, her narratives keep a focus on female lines of succession.

Methodius of Olympus' *Symposium, or On Chastity* was written approximately one hundred years after the *Acts of Paul and Thecla*. We do not know anything about Methodius' engagement with the cult of Thecla outside of the text: she is not brought up as an example in his other works, nor is she a recurring character in his philosophical dialogues, unlike some of his male characters. But Methodius was living and working on the southern coast of Lycia, not very far indeed from Myra, the location where Thecla was given permission to teach by Paul in the *Acts of Paul and Thecla*. Seleucia and its Thecla cult center were quite a bit further to the east (Davis 2008), but it would be surprising if there was not an active Thecla cult in Myra too, and in other locations in Lycia that were associated with her story.

Thecla is not Methodius' only female philosopher. Methodius' writings include a cluster of representations of intellectual women: the ten women in his *Symposium*, who are all "granddaughters" of Philosophy herself, the philosophically adept framing narrators Eubulion and Gregorion, Phrenope-Kalonia from the *De Cibis*, and "Philoxena" in the *De Lepra*. Methodius' works significantly expand our list of female philosophers from this time. This wider interest in female intellectual teachers helps explain why Methodius felt compelled to shift Thecla's characterization to that of philosopher.

2.2.1 The Philosophical Setting of the Symposium

Methodius of Olympus' *Symposium* opens with a dialogue between two women, one seeking to hear the story the other knows about a gathering of intellectual women. We will treat the characterization of these framing narrators, Gregorion and Eubulion, at the end of this section. But for now it is the cast list and scene-setting that are our focus. Gregorion is the first to tell us something about the event that she is about to describe. And that something has to do with philosophy.

> Gregorion: But first answer this question: do you know the daughter of
>   Philosophy – Arete?
> Eubulion: How could I not? (Meth. *Symp.* Prologue 4)[18]

> ΓΡΗΓ. Πρῶτον δέ μοι αὐτὴ ἀπόκριναι· γινώσκεις δήπου τὴν θυγατέρα
>   Φιλοσοφίας Ἀρετήν;
> ΕΥΒ. Τίοὖ;

In these first moments, we are told about the host and given a matronymic. Just like the introduction of Thecla in the *Acts of Paul and Thecla*, the female character's mother is given, with no mention of a father: Arete (Virtue), the daughter of Philosophy, is the owner of the garden to which the virgins are summoned. But this is not just any garden. It is a garden that is on top of a steep and treacherous mountain.

> What a rough and difficult path we traveled along, O Gregorion, and it was
> uphill too! (Meth. *Symp.* Prologue 5)

> Ὡς τραχεῖαν καὶ δύσβατον ὡδεύσαμεν, ὦ Γρηγόριον, καὶ ἀνάντη τρίβον.

---

[18] All translations of Methodius' *Symposium* are my own.

The path might be steep and treacherous, but it is not untraveled. Others had gone before them, and at the top, the heights of civilization await them with a fountain-decorated garden, delicious food and drink, all bathed in a gentle, flickering light. The perfect place to enjoy elite leisure activities such as philosophy.[19]

Virtue walks toward them with outstretched arms and greets them with the title of "daughters."

> This woman, coming to speak to each of us with great joy, our mother, just as if she was seeing us after a long time, hugged and kissed us, "Oh daughters . . . "
> (Meth. *Symp.* Prologue 9)

> Αὕτη οὖν προσελθοῦσα μετὰ πολλῆς χαρᾶς ἑκάστην ἡμῶν μήτηρ ὥσπερ διὰ πολλοῦ θεασαμένη περιεπτύσσετο καὶ κατεφίλει, Ὦ θυγατέρες . . .

That means that all of these women are symbolically granddaughters of Philosophy herself. It would be difficult to state more clearly that these women are being presented as philosophers, working in, at this point, an entirely female line of succession. As opposed to the quested after and eroticized Philosophy being the goal, as outlined in the Introduction, here Philosophy becomes a grandmother.

2.2.2 Thecla the Philosopher

Virtue is the daughter of Philosophy, and yet, rather than instigating an inquiry into truth via dialogue, she asks for something a bit more unexpected: speeches in praise of chastity (Meth. *Symp.* Prologue 9). Methodius' imitation of Plato's *Symposium* here makes this particular dialogue full of lengthy speeches rather than the back-and-forth of Methodius' other dialogues such as the *De Resurrectione*, the *De Autexusio*, and the *De Lepra*.

Seven other women give speeches to the approval of the gathered community before Thecla steps up for her turn. Thecla begins her contribution with a great amount of confidence. She claims for herself the wisdom of words (τὴν σοφίαν τῶν λόγων), and compares her soul to a stringed instrument, the cithara, harmonious and prepared for speaking in a practiced and orderly way (αἰσθανομένη κιθάρας δίκην ἔσωθεν ἁρμοζομένην με καὶ παρασκευάζουσαν εἰς τὸ μεμελημένως εἰπεῖν καὶ εὐσχημόνως, Meth. *Symp.* 7.9.169). Her focus on competition (ἀγωνίζεσθαι) and the metaphor of music have more resonances with rhetoric than philosophy.[20] The adverb she uses for how she speaks,

---

[19] Gardens as sites of philosophy were made famous through Epicurus' garden (Wycherley 1959), and this link has been suggested by Candido (Candido 2017, 113).

[20] It is sometimes difficult to distinguish philosophers from rhetoricians and sophists in the ancient world (Stanton 1973; Lauwers 2013).

"with care" (μεμελημένως, memelēmenōs), is also redolent of the schools, with their emphasis on declamations, which are called "things that you take care over" or *meletai* in Greek.

Virtue responds to Thecla's introduction by praising Thecla in telling terms:

> You are second to no one in philosophy and general education, as well as the evangelical and divine education, having been made wise by Paul, which is hardly necessary to say. (Meth. *Symp.* 7.9.170, my translation)

> Φιλοσοφίας τε γὰρ τῆς ἐγκυκλίου καὶ παιδείας οὐδενὸς ὑστερήσεις, τῆς εὐαγγελικῆς τε αὖ καὶ θείας τί χρὴ καὶ λέγειν, παρὰ Παύλῳ σεσοφισμένην;

"Philosophy" is placed at the very beginning of the sentence, emphasizing its importance to Thecla's characterization. But vitally, Virtue (who should know, since her mother is Philosophy) does not divorce philosophy from traditional education, asserting that Thecla has both.

This is a new addition to Thecla's characterization. As we examined above, in the *Acts of Paul and Thecla*, she was never called a philosopher, and she was not educated along traditional lines. We do not see her in school. Rather, she gets her credentials through withstanding trials and being a devoted follower of Christ. Methodius either knows of a different tradition or is inventing one in order to fit the context better, as well as reflecting the educated status of his female friends who read his work, as I will argue later on.

With such an introduction, we are led to hope that Thecla's speech will be special among the virgins. It is the longest, and even more interestingly, it comprises two separate speeches. Thecla first gives her speech in praise of chastity, as requested, but then asks for and receives permission to give a second speech. I will treat the philosophical nature of each in turn.

Her first speech begins with strong and persistent Platonic coloring. In the opening section, she gives two etymologies (of virginity and of virtue, Meth. *Symp.* 8.1.171), a favorite Platonic move, and then moves on to rewrite the myth of ascending with the wings of the soul found in the *Phaedrus* (Meth. *Symp.* 8.1.172–8.3.179). Twice she refers to this life as the true drama (Meth. *Symp.* 8.1.172 and 8.2.173), perhaps nodding to the dramatic version of philosophy popularized by Socratic dialogues.

These are some of the links to the Platonic dialogic tradition, but the Platonic emphasis continues in her overarching theme of this section – the stratification of reality. Thecla is unabashedly an idealist: she argues that the current world is a shadow of the real world to come. Only in the next world will one be able to encounter "Justice itself, and Love itself, and Truth and Prudence and all the other flowers and plants of Wisdom in like splendor, of which we in this world see merely ghost-like shadows as in a dream" (Meth. *Symp.* 8.3.177). While on earth, in the realm of shadows, the mind's functions of thought and imagination allow humans to participate in the real realm proleptically.[21] Intellectual activities such as the philosophical discussion among the women and Methodius' writing of the dialogic text are fundamental to the task of keeping attention focused in the right direction.

The main body of Thecla's first speech, like that of the virgins, is exegetical. But the exegesis is supported by a wide array of knowledge taken from other branches of learning. She chooses as her primary passage for commentary Revelation 12, the story of the woman clothed in the sun. She starts by admitting that the text includes many enigmas, but she proclaims that she is undaunted by the exegetical task (Meth. *Symp.* 8.9.194). Her exegesis of the elements of the biblical story focus on the role of the moon (Meth. *Symp.* 8.6.186–87) and the stars (Meth. *Symp.* 8.10.196). This leads naturally to her proposition to Virtue to give another speech about astrology once she has completed her encomium to chastity. In addition to interpreting the heavenly bodies, Thecla also includes a section of numerology, showing how a correct grasp of arithmetic is also necessary to the life chosen by these virgins of biblical interpretation (Meth. *Symp.* 8.11.197–203). Finally, she ends her speech with a small poem that she composed through rewriting Homer's *Iliad* 6.18–183 and changing its meaning by adding two new lines of dactylic hexameter of her own invention (Meth. *Symp.* 8.12.205). Thecla, then, at the service of exegesis, shows expert knowledge in Platonic texts, astrology, mathematics, and poetry.

After completing her contribution that shows her wide education in the liberal arts, she asks to follow with a second speech specifically to refute the astronomers on the topic of free will. Dylan Burns, in investigating the astronomical arguments in Thecla's second speech, reminds us that Thecla's excursus on the stars is a philosophical discussion about free will, determinism, and desire (Burns 2017). Methodius cares deeply about these topics and wrote an entire work discussing free will, the *De Autexusio*.[22] Thecla's second speech shows how mathematics and astronomy are subsets of philosophy that can further illuminate other aspects of philosophy such as anthropology and ethics. Her speeches give evidence of a range of technical training that has been put at the service of philosophical argumentation about the nature of the universe and humanity's place within it.

---

[21] "But they achieve the assembly of those already in heaven through their discursive thought and the impulse of their desire" (ἀλλὰ τῷ φρονήματι καὶ τῇ ὁρμῇ τῆς ἐπιθυμίας εἰς τὴν ἄγυριν ἤδη τῶν ἐν τοῖς οὐρανοῖς τυγχάνειν. Meth. *Symp.* 8.2.174).

[22] Some scholars think that Thecla's second speech is a digest of Methodius' *De Autexusio* that sits uneasily appended to the *Symposium*, but Burns wishes to place it more firmly within the narrative interests of this work (Burns 2017, 210, 217–20).

When Thecla asks Virtue permission to expand her speech, Virtue grants it because of an argument of fittingness. She says that Thecla's speech will be perfectly adorned (τελέως γὰρ ὁ λόγος κεκοσμήσεται) if the astronomical discussions are attached (Meth. *Symp.* 8.13.210). The language here is one of adornment, which would at first blush seem to link this section more with rhetoric than with philosophy. However, there is also a play on words here. When Virtue claims that Thecla's speech will be properly adorned if she attaches a discussion about the stars, Thecla responds by immediately repeating the terminology of adornment, linking the word adorn (*kosmeo*) to the word for universe (*kosmos*). She makes a knowing pun on the link between cosmetology and cosmology before launching into an anti-determinism argument in which she reveals her astrological knowledge. Her technical scientific knowledge is put to the service of a philosophical argument about anthropology and fate.

She starts by calling astrology witchcraft (γοητεία), disassociating it from true wisdom or philosophy. In particular, she connects astrology with Chaldean knowledge (Meth. *Symp.* 8.13.210). But although Thecla references Chaldean knowledge, with its associations with eastern mysticism, when she goes on to describe the motions of the earth and the stars, she uses terminology that has its origin in Ptolemy's *Almagest*, the extremely popular work of mathematical astronomy written in Alexandria in the mid-second century CE.

Ptolemy's introduction to his work places the study of the motion of the heavenly bodies at the center of philosophy. Among the three subsections of theoretical philosophy enumerated by Aristotle (*Metaphysics* E 1.1026a.18ff) of theology, mathematics, and physics, Ptolemy argues that only mathematics is certain. Theology has to do with things we cannot know, and physics is too wrapped up in the changing world to provide certain knowledge. But mathematics has as its object the motion of the heavenly bodies which are both unchanging and observable. Mathematics provides insight into both theology and physics, while the same cannot be said in the other direction (*Almagest* 1.1, H7-H8; Ptolemy 1998, 35–36). According to Ptolemy, then, the mathematics of astronomy are the truest form of philosophy.

A true understanding of the cosmos, accordingly, requires correct knowledge of mathematics. Thecla asserts that astronomers only *claim* to be mathematical, while teaching evil doctrines of astral determinism (τὴν μαθηματικὴν ταύτην μᾶλλον δὲ καταθεματικὴν πρόγνωσιν, Meth. *Symp.* 8.15.216). She has earlier shown her own agility with numbers in the numerological interpretation of the biblical passage. Thecla tries to demonstrate what true mathematical knowledge looks like in the face of the false mathematics of the astronomers. She not only has a solid education in the liberal arts but she also knows how to use it to support correctly ordered ideas of cosmology and anthropology. In her speech in praise of chastity, she contests various forms of knowledge and the ways in which they fit into a larger philosophical system.

2.2.3 Methodius' Frame and Methodius the Author (Methodius in Drag)

The ten women philosophers who give speeches at Virtue's behest are not the only philosophical women in the dialogue. There are also two feminine framing narrators, Gregorion and Eubulion, who tell the story and are told the story respectively. They play roles at four points: in the opening, at two points of interruption during the competition, and in a final lengthy debate about desire after the symposium of the virgins concludes. The beginning characterization sets Eubulion against Gregorion as a teasing interlocutor who cares more about a good story than about the truth. But at the end, we get a more developed characterization of the two women, including some specific connections to the philosophical life.

Eubulion's patient listening to the long tale told her by Gregorion ends in her instigating a philosophical debate with her former teacher. Eubulion goes from passive recipient to the originator of a new track of conversation: is it better to feel no desire, or to experience desire and overcome it? Gregorion believes that it is better to have no desire, but her opinion (and confidence) are soon undermined by Eubulion's questioning.

> Eubulion: Don't say that, my dear lady! For I am amazed at your intelligence and your high-mindedness. I was saying this because you are claiming that you not only understand but even are proud enough to teach to others things that many wise men have often argued about with each other.
>
> (Meth. *Symp.* Epilogue 294–95)
>
> ΕΥΒ. Εὐφήμησον, ὦ μακαρία· θαυμάζω γὰρ σφόδρα σου τὸ συνετὸν καὶ μεγαλόδοξον. Ἐγὼ τοῦτο ἔφην ὅτι περὶ ὧν πολλοὶ πρὸς ἑαυτοὺς πολλάκις ἀμφισβητοῦσι σοφοί, ταῦτα οὐ μόνον ἐπίστασθαι σὺ λέγεις ἀλλὰ καὶ διδάσκειν ἑτέρους σεμνύνῃ.

Eubulion claims that Gregorion has given herself airs as a teacher (διδάσκειν ἑτέρους σεμνύνῃ) and continues to undercut her with persistent questioning until at the end Gregorion suggests that they resume their conversation the next day. Only this time, she will be learning from Eubulion rather than the other way around. Women can teach other women, and those female students can also then take on the role of teachers, displaying in sometimes disconcerting ways how they themselves have become experts in dialectic.

There are female teachers throughout the *Symposium*, from Virtue herself to Thecla, and out into the framing narrators. But the all-female space created in the dialogue keeps the teaching of women safely between women. Are men involved in this teaching network? If so, only in a sly way.

Methodius, as a character in his own dialogues, goes by two names. In the same dialogue, he can be called both Methodius and Eubulius. We see a similar dynamic in Methodius' letter-treatise *De Cibis*, where the same addressee is variously called Phrenope and Kalonia. I would suggest that Phrenope ("brainy") might be a nickname for Kalonia, in a similar way that Eubulius ("good-council") might be a nickname for Methodius (LaValle Norman 2019b, 97; Bracht 1999, 177–78).[23] A further complication, however, is introduced in the *Symposium* when a character is called Eubul-ion, the feminine diminutive of Eubul-ius.[24] Musurillo suggests that this is a female cipher for Methodius (Musurillo 1963, 95:42). Then, the witty listener who bests her/his interlocutor at the end would be none other than our author himself, in drag.

What makes the identification between Eubulion and Methodius even stranger is that Methodius does make himself a minor "off-stage" character in the dialogue.[25]

> Eubulion: And what then? Tell me whether our Telmessian friend wasn't outside listening? For I am amazed if she kept her peace, having learned about this gathering and not immediately set her mind to hearing what was said, just like a bird swooping down for food.
>
> Gregorion: No. The story goes that she was standing next to Methodius when he was asking Virtue about these things. It's a good and blessed thing to have such a teacher and guide as Virtue!
>
> (Meth. *Symp.* Epilogue 293)

> ΕΥΒ. Τί δαί; ἡ Τελμησσιακὴ ξένη, εἰπέ μοι, κἂν ἔξωθεν οὐκ ἐπηκροᾶτο; Θαυμάζω γὰρ εἰ ἡσυχίαν εἶχεν ἐκείνη μαθοῦσα τὸ συσσίτιον τοῦτο καὶ οὐκ εὐθέως ὥσπερ ὄρνεον ἐπὶ τροφὴν ἐφίπτατο τῶν λεγομένων ἀκουσομένη.
>
> ΓΡΗΓ. Οὔ· λόγος γὰρ αὐτὴν Μεθοδίῳ συμπαραγεγονέναι αὐτὰ δὴ ταῦτα τὴν Ἀρετὴν πυνθανομένῳ. Ἀλλὰ καλὸν καὶ μακάριον τοιαύτῃ διδασκάλῳ χρήσασθαι καὶ ὁδηγῷ τῇ Ἀρετῇ.

At the end, Gregorion tells Eubulion that Methodius heard it directly from Virtue herself, whom he interviewed about the matter. In that off-stage scene,

---

[23] Some scholars think that there are two separate women addressed in the *De Cibis* (DePalma Digeser 2017, 146–47; Patterson 1997, 27). I find it more likely that this is a double naming of one woman. In the opening paragraph, Methodius addresses only Phrenope, and it would be odd to dedicate a work to two women without mentioning them both in the opening (*De Cibis* 1.1). Phrenope could easily be a nickname for Kilonia meaning "brainy." In his translation of the *De Cibis* from the Old Church Slavonic and entered in the public domain, Ralph Cleminson remains agnostic on the issue, saying of the name Kilonia "the underlying Greek cannot be deduced with any certainty, nor is it certain whether this is the same person as the Phrenope addressed at the beginning of the work" (Methodius of Olympus 2015, n.20).

[24] Clearly, this caused confusion in readers throughout time: multiple manuscripts transform the feminine diminutive Eubulion into the masculine Eubulios (Musurillo 1963, 95:42–43, n.1).

[25] Causing Musurillo to suggest that he "forgot" that he had already scripted himself into the dialogue as a woman (Musurillo 1963, 95:42).

we see that Virtue can be the best and most direct teacher. Yet, "Methodius" still remains "outside" (ἔξωθεν) the event. Oddly, Eubulion had not even asked after Methodius, but Gregorion mentions him in such a way that he is apparently known to both of them. Perhaps this was precisely to get around the odd situation of Eubulion asking after her alter ego.

Federica Candido has gathered an excellent set of references to the "school of virtue" as a phrase for Christian educational establishments in the third and fourth centuries, some particularly open to women students and women teachers (Candido 2017, 108–14). Methodius plays on this phrase and makes the "school of virtue" a concrete name, de-allegorizing it and translating it into the "school of the woman named Virtue." When he shifts "virtue" from being a noun to being a proper name, he heightens the gendered aspects of the phrase, and allows not only the women in the story to be students of female Virtue but also the male Methodius, even if he desires to maintain gender-segregated "classrooms."

2.2.4 Conclusion

Methodius was an author interested in female teachers across multiple works. We have focused here on the *Symposium* because it features the character of Thecla. In addition to his *Symposium*, though, he also quotes the words of a wise female teacher named Philoxena in his dialogue the *De Lepra* (Meth. *De Lep.* 13.1–5), and he corresponds with Phrenope-Kalonia, a woman whose ideas he appreciates and whom he says shares his life of philosophy (Methodius *De Cibis* 4.2). The combination of all of these shows Methodius to be an author very interested in presenting himself as a friend to philosophical women, providing the larger context for his transformation of Thecla from itinerant preacher to philosopher. After all, Methodius' own internal readers in the *Symposium*, Eubulion and Gregorion, admit to being awed by the story of Thecla. We will see in the next example, Macrina, that later Christian women were also inspired by her and, in particular, by Methodius' assertion that she was a philosopher.

Thecla's change from itinerant charismatic preacher in the *Acts* to philosopher and rhetorician in the *Symposium* matches the change in genre and the change in era. Methodius typified Thecla as a philosopher primarily by moving her into a philosophical genre, and then letting her behave accordingly. He connects the life of philosophy with the life of virtue and asceticism but adds in the assumption of a liberal arts education. Thecla displays wide knowledge spanning from poetic composition to mathematical symbolism to scientific astronomy, all put to the service of biblical interpretation and supporting the life of chastity. Thecla thereby becomes a model of an intellectual life that includes study, asceticism, and rational dialogue.

I argue, furthermore, that these philosophical women were not only meant to inspire female readers. Methodius depicts the male version of himself as an eager listener to the story about the virgins' rhetorical competition in the *Symposium*, and Sistelius is happy to depict himself as a student of "Philoxena" in Methodius' *De Lep.* 13.1–5. Perhaps the classrooms are not quite as gender-segregated as they first appeared. Even beyond this, the *Symposium* includes a deeper argument for imaginatively "becoming female" at the biological/allegorical level. The ideal Christian, whether male or female, is encouraged to view their ideal lives as pregnant, birthing, and nursing mothers (LaValle Norman 2019a), which Methodius aligns with a life of philosophical discussion, twisting the Platonic metaphor from the *Symposium* into new, and more truly feminine, directions.

2.3 Conclusion

The anonymous *Acts of Paul and Thecla* and Methodius of Olympus' *Symposium* both feature Thecla as their star character and build their narrative upon related characterizations. In both texts, Thecla is scripted as a female teacher and enlightener in ways that are unexpected for female characters of her time. Yet she also performs in a female way, especially in her persistent characterization as a daughter: whether that is a biological daughter of Theocleia or a spiritual daughter of Tryphaena in the *Acts of Paul and Thecla*, or a metaphorical daughter of Virtue in the *Symposium*.

Thecla represents educational leadership in the context of predominantly female sociality. Although she is the student of Paul in the *Acts of Paul and Thecla* and has both male and female disciples after her transition to itinerant preacher, it is still her "mothers" who feature most prominently. Similarly, the male listener to the story told in the *Symposium* (who is Methodius himself) is only allowed access in a roundabout way: the main relationships are between philosophical women who have been summoned by a female host to an all-female party. The next philosopher we will turn to had a more gender-diverse influence.

Yet, the importance of these female circles of influence should not be understated. Thecla in her *Acts*, although taking on some masculine characteristics, remains female in important ways, and the pathways to piety she points to for people like Tryphaena or her own mother are distinctly feminine modes of holiness. Likewise in the *Symposium*, the women are more often encouraged to imitate female models rather than "become male." While we do not see in the Thecla stories much emphasis on women teaching men, women are allowed to express their holiness through feminine characteristics, rather than by overcoming them, allowed to "stay female" rather than "become male" in the growth toward perfection (LaValle Norman 2019a).

3 Macrina the Younger, "Who Raised Herself to the Furthest Limit of Human Virtue through Philosophy" (Greg. Nyss. *Vit. Macr.* 1.27–29)

When we move from Thecla to our next example, Macrina, many scholars would claim that we move broadly from the realm of myth to the realm of history. However, a strong dichotomy between myth and history is problematic with these sources. Thecla, Macrina, and Monica are all "written" women, with precious little evidence beyond the texts analyzed in this Element.[26] And "mythical" women, like Thecla, were often very real to other ancient people. For instance, Thecla's legend was thought by Gregory of Nyssa to have made a direct impact on his mother and sister in ways that I will explore further below.

There is no doubt in her ancient biographer's mind that Macrina was a philosopher. Gregory of Nyssa repeatedly calls his sister a philosopher, with a density of vertical phrases centered around the concept of the "heights of philosophy." This recurring image links Macrina to the ascent myths outlined in the Introduction.

Gregory wrote of his sister in depth in two texts, which characterize her somewhat differently due to different expectations caused by their genre. The first is a biography, *The Life of Macrina*, moving in the traditional order from her birth to some events occurring after her death. There are some moments of direct speech in the *Life*, but the only extended moment of Macrina in "verbal mode" in this text is her prayer of thanksgiving on her deathbed, rather than a clear display of philosophical teaching. The second text is a philosophical dialogue between Macrina and her brother-author, which depicts a zoom-in of one of the moments that was only narrated in indirect speech in the biography. This dialogue is titled *On the Soul and Resurrection*. While these two texts about Macrina are often conglomerated, I think that they need to be carefully separated (LaValle Norman 2023). Macrina's philosophical abilities are presented differently in the two texts in correspondence to the different choice of genre. In particular, there is a significant difference in the valuation of secular knowledge.

3.1 The *Life of Macrina*: A Philosopher on the Move at Home

The *Life of Macrina* is a biography of a woman explicitly styled as a philosopher.[27] But not only does she herself personally lack traditional education, she even

---

[26] Gregory of Nyssa also talks about the death of his sister closer to the actual event in Letter 19. Monica's epitaph in Ostia was probably not a contemporary monument, but a later attempt to promote 'pious tourism' (Boin 2010).

[27] Urbano argues that Macrina represents a new type of education that is apart from the ancient course of education. "In Greek biographies, the unlettered subject served to validate and reinforce pedagogic institutions, while in the Christian biographies, unschooled subjects served

implies that such education gets in the way of true philosophy. Rather than focusing on words, philosophy is presented spatially, as an ascent to a higher form of life that is beyond the material, on the border with the life of the angels. Such a philosophy allows one to speak in an orderly manner (rather than in the way practiced by those who are puffed up with rhetorical training, such as Macrina's brother Basil upon his return from Athens, Greg. Nyss. *Vit. Macr.* 8.1 Silvas/6 Maraval), but the focus is not verbal.

Gregory opens his book about his sister with the question of genre and the theme of excess. He tells his unnamed dedicatee that the heading makes his work look like a letter, but the reality is much greater. The subject matter demanded a longer treatment than a letter could afford, and so by its nature it expanded into a "lengthy narrative" (εἰς συγγραφικὴν μακρηγορίαν, Greg. Nyss. *Vit. Macr.* 1.1 Silvas/1 Maraval). Gregory's letter grew beyond the initial limits set for it (ὑπὲρ τὸν ἐπιστολιμαῖον ὅρον, Greg. Nyss. *Vit. Macr.* 1.1 Silvas/1 Maraval), breaking the requirements of the genre. Gregory's excessive letter matches its content: Macrina is a woman who went beyond the limits of her nature (Greg. Nyss. *Vit. Macr.* 1.5 Silvas/1 Maraval). Yet, despite its excessiveness, Gregory says that his story will be written without artifice and simply (ἐν ἀκατασκεύῳ τε καὶ ἁπλῷ διηγήματι). This too echoes Macrina's characterization. Her excessive life is crafted without any of the artifice provided by a secular education and demonstrates the simplicity learned through a new Christian education.

3.1.1 Methodius' Thecla as Macrina's Philosophical Model

Gregory constructs Macrina's story as one of movement, and the constant theme running throughout the text is journeying to what is "above." Gregory tells us that he was encouraged to write this biography so that a woman, "veiled in silence," might not be unprofitably neglected, a woman who "through philosophy had lifted herself to the highest summit of human virtue" (πρὸς τὸν ἀκρότατον τῆς ἀνθρωπίνης ἀρετῆς ὅρον ἑαυτὴν διὰ φιλοσοφίας ἐπάρασα Greg. Nyss. *Vit Macr.* 1.5 Silvas/1 Maraval). Apparently, there are some feminine veils that are inappropriate, and Gregory will remove this one by writing his sister's biography. Ultimately, Macrina will go above her nature; she will become angelic (Greg. Nyss. *Vit. Macr.* 1.3 Silvas/1 Maraval). Yet, as lived by humans, this life is in between, "methorios": angelic even while still within the body (Daniélou 1961).

The prefatory opening is the first time that Gregory uses a recurrent image in the biography, connecting philosophy with height. Here, it is not only height,

---

to negotiate competing Christian positions on the place of *paideia* and present cases for degrees of dislocating 'philosophy' from categories of ethnicity, culture, and gender" (Urbano 2013, 256).

but the highest limit (τὸν ἀκρότατον . . . ὅρον), echoing the limits that Gregory's text exceeds as well. These limits both make a parallel between Gregory's excessive text and Macrina's excessive life, and bring in a sense of verticality by looking suspiciously like mountain peaks. With the flip of a breathing mark, the limit (ὅρον) becomes a mountain (ὄρον). And if that were to happen, Gregory no longer tells us that Macrina achieved the highest limit of human virtue (ἀρετῆς ὅρον), but that she made it to the very top of the Mountain of Virtue (Ἀρετῆς ὄρον).[28] From this opening summary, a suspicion arises that Methodius' *Symposium* might be in the background of Gregory of Nyssa's philosophical depiction of his sister.

This suspicion is intensified when he moves to the first biographical section of his text, about Macrina's name. Although her formal name was Macrina, after her paternal grandmother Macrina the Elder, her mother gave her the private family name of Thecla at her birth (Greg. Nyss. *Vit Macr.* 3.2 Silvas/2 Maraval).

Gregory does not tell us how her mother knew about Thecla and her story. As we discussed in the last section, Thecla's story was preserved both in biographical form in the *Acts of Paul and Thecla* and in dialogue form in Methodius' *Symposium*. Most commonly, scholars have looked to the more famous narrative of Thecla's life for answers to the secret name (Urbano 2013, 264), or to links with an active Thecla cult in Asia Minor rather than textual knowledge (Davis 2008, 62–64). However, a collection of authors have argued instead that it would make more sense for Macrina's Thecla to be Methodius' Thecla, creating a line of female *philosophers* (Albrecht 1986; Silvas 2008, 17–20).

I agree that Gregory is trying to activate our memories of Methodius' *Symposium* and think that there might be even more details that support this reading. The first I have already explained: the "limit" of virtue can become the Mountain of Virtue with the flip of a breathing mark. The second is in the way that Gregory describes Thecla when the secret name is introduced:

ἐκείνης Θέκλης, ἧς πολὺς ἐν ταῖς παρθένοις ὁ λόγος.

(Greg. Nyss. *Vit. Macr.* 3.2 Silvas/2 Maraval)

The way that this has been translated is "that Thecla whose fame is so great among the virgins" (Silvas 2008, 112), and that is certainly the normal way of taking this line. But because *logos* is such a polyvalent word in Greek, it could also mean, "Thecla, whose speech was long among the virgins." If so, then it would be a *double entendre*, reminding those in the know of Methodius' *Symposium*, where Thecla does indeed give the longest speech of all the virgins.

---

[28] Gregory uses the phrase "limit of virtue" twice in the *Life of Moses* (1.7 and 1.8), and the "mountain of virtue" is found in Quintus Smyrnaeus (Maciver 2007).

But just as the name was kept secret from the public and only circulated among the family, so too would the hidden import only strike the educated reader who knew Methodius' text, like the Mountain of Virtue hiding in plain sight.

In the midst of these literary relationships, we must also remember that Thecla had an active shrine nearby where Macrina's family lived. Family and friends would have visited this shrine and been in touch with the living tradition active there. It was to the shrine of Thecla in Seleucia that Gregory Nazianzus, Gregory of Nyssa's friend, fled his political episcopal obligations (Hayne 1994, 212; McGuckin 2001, 229–30). The interaction between these traditions was not only literary but also at the level of material cult.

3.1.2 Macrina's Education

Immediately after explaining the connection between Macrina and Thecla, Gregory continues with a narration of Macrina's education. This ends when she turns twelve years old, which was the legal minimum for marriage in the Roman Empire (Shaw 1987, 42), although not the standard age of marriage. From that point on, the narrative moves to discussing the plans for her marriage (Greg. Nyss. *Vit. Macr.* 5.1 Silvas/4 Maraval). Her education was guided by her *mother* (Ἦν δὲ τῇ μητρὶ σπουδὴ παιδεῦσαι μὲν τὴν παῖδα, Greg. Nyss. *Vit. Macr.* 4.2 Silvas/3 Maraval), continuing the strong mother–daughter educational bonds that we have already observed in the Thecla literature.

We are first told what her education was *not*: it was precisely not a "liberal arts" education (ἐγκύκλιον παίδευσιν) of the sort that Methodius' *Symposium* claimed for Thecla (μὴ μέντοι τὴν ἔξωθεν ταύτην καὶ ἐγκύκλιον παίδευσιν, Greg. Nyss. *Vit. Macr.* 4.2 Silvas/3 Maraval). Macrina's mother avoided the poetry of Homer and the tragedians that formed the basis of secular education, but she did not avoid poetry entirely. Macrina was taught to recite the Psalms throughout the day. In addition to this type of poetry, the other "substitutions" for a secular education were the moral lessons of the Wisdom of Solomon and the training of manual labor (askēsasa/ἀσκήσασα, linking it to the ascetical life she would later develop, Greg. Nyss. *Vit. Macr.* 5.1 Silvas/4 Maraval).

Gregory removes any possibility of secular learning from Macrina's biography. She is kept from the standards of education, guided up a path that focuses on the development of the moral life (τὸν ἠθικὸν βίον, Greg. Nyss. *Vit. Macr.* 4.3 Silvas/3 Maraval) rather than the intellectual life. There is no verbal connection in the description of her education with a life of philosophy. Rather, that is reserved for later in the narrative.

3.1.3 Heights of Philosophy

The limits of virtue to which philosophy permitted Macrina to ascend recalled Methodius' depiction of Thecla as a mountain-dwelling philosopher at the very outset of the narrative. But Gregory pulls the connection of philosophy and height into the rest of his narrative as well. The thorough-going metaphor of height and philosophy is unmistakable. For instance, Gregory describes how Macrina led her brother Peter to "the high goal of philosophy" (πρὸς τὸν ὑψηλὸν τῆς φιλοσοφίας σκοπὸν, Greg. Nyss. *Vit. Macr.* 14.3 Silvas/12 Maraval), and likewise he describes Macrina and Peter's continued life after their mother's death as pursuing the higher part of philosophy (Οἱ δὲ πληρώσαντες τὸ διατεταγμένον ὑψηλότερον εἴχοντο τῆς φιλοσοφίας, Greg. Nyss. *Vit. Macr.* 15.5 Silvas/13 Maraval).

There are two sections of the *Life of Macrina* that are particularly rich in the vocabulary of philosophy and deserve further study in order to determine what Gregory understood by the terms that he applies to Macrina and her way of life.

In the first, Gregory describes how as her mother grew older, Macrina was able to lead them both ever deeper into a life of philosophy (Greg. Nyss. *Vit. Macr.* 13 Silvas/11 Maraval). First, Gregory sets off their new life by mentioning how it was made possible by the cessation of the physical duties of Macrina's mother. Only when she finished raising her ten children was she able to start living a philosophical life. The lack of material concerns is a prerequisite. It is nearly a synonym: Gregory connects the life of philosophy with the alpha-privative adjective ἄϋλον, non-material, twice in the work.[29]

> Then, just as was said before, the life of the virgin became an advisor of her mother for how to lead life philosophically and nonmaterially ...
>
> (Greg. Nyss. *Vit. Macr.* 13.1 Silvas/11 Maraval)

> ... τότε, καθὼς προείρηται, γίνεται σύμβουλος τῆς μητρὸς ἡ τῆς παρθένου ζωὴ πρὸς τὴν ἐμφιλόσοφον ταύτην καὶ ἄϋλον τοῦ βίου διαγωγὴν ...

It does not seem that her mother would have been able to have combined the busy life of a wife and mother with the philosophical life. One needed to cease before another could commence.

Mother and daughter leave behind their responsibilities of care, anxiety, status, luxury, distinction, desire for glory, luxury, and wealth. With these distractions removed, they turn their focus onto noetic concerns. Gregory explains the content of their philosophical life with an ascending triad: meditation on divine things, unceasing prayer, and uninterrupted hymnody throughout the day and night (μόνη δὲ ἡ τῶν θείων μελέτη καὶ τὸ τῆς προσευχῆς

---

[29] The word "non-material" (ἄϋλον) is a favorite for Gregory, and he uses it over forty times in his corpus, often in conjunction with "noetic."

ἀδιάλειπτον καὶ ἡ ἄπαυστος ὑμνῳδία, Greg. Nyss. *Vit. Macr.* 13.5 Silvas/11
Maraval). While all of these actions are noetic rather than physical, they do not
fit into the traditional understanding of philosophy that would be found in the
school curriculum. In fact, it is a definition of philosophy that is explicitly
counter to secular education. The following section outlines how Macrina took
her youngest brother Peter's education in hand and kept him away from
"profane literary studies" (τοὺς ἔξωθεν τῶν λόγων), educating him instead in
sacred learning (ἐπὶ πᾶσαν τὴν ὑψηλοτέραν ἤγαγε παίδευσιν, τοῖς ἱεροῖς τῶν
μαθημάτων, Greg. Nyss. *Vit. Macr.* 14.2 Silvas/12 Maraval). This redefinition
makes philosophy something that is not only *apart* from secular learning, but
even in direct opposition.[30]

The conflict had already been cemented in the previous section, which
narrated Basil's return home at the end of his rhetorical training. His rhetorical
training is not described as philosophy, or even as preparatory for philosophy.
Instead, it is described as having a completely different goal, which Macrina
must lead him away from in order that he might advance toward the goal of
philosophy (τοσούτῳ τάχει κἀκεῖνον πρὸς τὸν τῆς φιλοσοφίας σκοπὸν
ἐπεσπάσατο, Greg. Nyss. *Vit. Macr.* 8.3 Silvas/6 Maraval).

The second central passage to understand Gregory's use of philosophy in the
Life of Macrina covers the same period of time as the dialogue that we will look
at next. Gregory has come home to find his sister on her deathbed. Macrina
starts the conversation with recollecting Basil, whose funeral had just occurred.
Macrina makes Basil's death "a starting point for the higher philosophy" (ὥστε
ἀφορμὴν ποιησαμένη τῆς ὑψηλοτέρας φιλοσοφίας, Greg. Nyss. *Vit. Macr.* 20.1
Silvas/17 Maraval). We are immediately put into the familiar metaphorical
space equating philosophy with height. Gregory first confesses that all of him
was low at the memory of Basil's death: his soul was low, his face was fallen,
and tears were coming down. He says even his soul was bent on one knee (ἐμοὶ
μὲν ἐπώκλαζεν ἡ ψυχή, Greg. Nyss. *Vit. Macr.* 20.1 Silvas/17 Maraval).
Gregory is down and going lower.

Macrina, through her conversation, brings him up to philosophy. And they do
not stop in the middle but ascend beyond the human – or at least it *seems* that
way, to be more precise about Gregory's diction here.

> So that my soul seemed to be separated for a little while outside of human
> nature, raised up by what she was saying and set down within the heavenly
> places, by the manuduction of her speech.
>
>   (Greg. Nyss. *Vit. Macr.* 20.2 Silvas/17 Maraval)

---

[30] Malingrey concludes, looking at texts besides the *Life of Macrina*, that Gregory primarily uses
"philosophy" to refer to the ascetic life (Malingrey 1961, 257–61).

ὥστε μοι τὴν ψυχὴν ἔξω μικροῦ δεῖν τῆς ἀνθρωπίνης φύσεως εἶναι δοκεῖν συνεπαρθεῖσαν τοῖς λεγομένοις καὶ ἐντὸς τῶν οὐρανίων ἀδύτων τῇ χειραγωγίᾳ τοῦ λόγου καθισταμένην.

Macrina takes Gregory by the hand, allegorically (τῇ χειραγωγίᾳ), to raise him up from the downward trajectory on which he was stuck with Basil's death, and bring him back to standing, and even beyond to heights he had not yet reached. The vertical metaphors are endemic.

Unlike in the first passage, here Gregory narrates a type of Macrinian philosophizing that could fit into "professional" definitions. In fact, there are four things that Gregory lays out as the content of Macrina's philosophizing during this deathbed conversation, which sound very much like the content of Plato's *Phaedo*.

> But if it hadn't been that my writing would be stretched out to limitless size, I would have gone through everything in order, how she was raised up by discourse, philosophizing to us about the soul, the cause of life through the flesh, for what reason a human exists, how a human is mortal, whence comes death and what release there is from this into life again.
>
> (Greg. Nyss. *Vit Macr.* 20.5 Silvas/18 Maraval)

Καὶ εἰ μὴ πρὸς ἄπειρον ἐξετείνετο μῆκος ἡ συγγραφή, πάντα ἂν καθεξῆς διηγησάμην, ὅπως ἐπήρθη τῷ λόγῳ περί τε τῆς ψυχῆς ἡμῖν φιλοσοφοῦσα καὶ τῆς διὰ σαρκὸς ζωῆς τὴν αἰτίαν διεξιοῦσα, καὶ ὅτου χάριν ὁ ἄνθρωπος καὶ ὅπως θνητὸς καὶ ὅθεν ὁ θάνατος καὶ τίς ἡ ἀπὸ τούτου πρὸς τὴν ζωὴν πάλιν ἀνάλυσις.

These can be broken down into the following four topics:

1. "About the soul" (περί τε τῆς ψυχῆς): We have many ancient treatises that go under this title. Of greatest interest here is that it was the subtitle of Plato's *Phaedo* and was known to many ancients under that name.

2. "The cause of life through the flesh and for what reason a human exists" (τῆς διὰ σαρκὸς ζωῆς τὴν αἰτίαν ὅτου χάριν ὁ ἄνθρωπος). Macrina's philosophy takes a biological turn, explaining how humans come into existence. There were various philosophical works "on generation," the most famous from the Hippocratic corpus. But Gregory says that Macrina links this with questions of meaning and the ends of human existence.

3. "How man is mortal and whence comes death" (ὅτου χάριν ὁ ἄνθρωπος καὶ ὅπως θνητὸς καὶ ὅθεν ὁ θάνατος). Following up on her interest in humans coming into existence is her interest in the flip side, human death.

4. "What is the release from this back to life" (τίς ἡ ἀπὸ τούτου πρὸς τὴν ζωὴν πάλιν ἀνάλυσις). Here comes the surprise. Macrina's philosophical discourse ends with discussing the return to life after death.

Yet, all of the summarized content of her speech is given in indirect discourse. Gregory follows this with one line of direct discourse from his sister, where she tells him to take a rest after his long journey. Gregory decides not to write a biography that includes lengthy, content-rich speeches from his sister. Rather, her philosophical life is demonstrated via other means, such as the practical and humble concern of sister for brother.

Gregory admitted upfront that his biography exceeded its limits. If this is already the case, what harm would there be in adding a bit more? Why repeat the concern here that any further addition would make the text "limitless" (πρὸς ἄπειρον . . . μῆκος)? He has already made his peace with exceeding the bounds of the epistolary genre. Perhaps, though, he could not reconcile inserting a lengthy philosophical dialogue into his biography because of the way that it would affect the characterization of his sister's wisdom, a wisdom which he has worked so hard in the rest of the dialogue to divorce from secular learning.

While the philosophical life as demonstrated by Gregory's Macrina in the *Life of Macrina* may seem like an inclusive definition of philosophy, it remains exclusive, just along different axes. No expensive education is required, but one must be able to leave all obligations behind, which means that those living in the thick of marriage and child-rearing are unsuitable. Gregory narrates how Macrina brought many of her family members into her life of philosophy. Her mother and at least three of her brothers (four if you count the author, which you must) are described as leading a life of philosophy in their family home. We do not hear how she led her five sisters into a life of philosophy. Instead, we hear that their mother found ways of life that suited them (Greg. Nyss. *Vit. Macr.* 8.1 Silvas/6 Maraval). Presumably, this would be suitable marriages, which means that they would temporarily be cut off from living a life of philosophy because their obligations would not permit it. They were bound to live a practical life, perhaps with the hope of joining the philosophical household establishment once their children were taken care of, as had been the case with their lucky mother.

3.1.4 Macrina's Prayer

Gregory's characterization of Macrina in biographical mode focuses on her religious, liturgical relationship with God rather than the discursive and dialogic interactions. It is for this reason that Anna Silvas suggests "mystagogy" as the genre of the work, noting the liturgical valence of many of the scenes of Macrina's life (Silvas 2008, 104–8). Gregory's *Life of Macrina* avoids record-ing Macrina's words at key places. Gregory says that doing so would extend his work too much – the theme of excess with which he opened the dedication letter is here instantiated once again, but this time he keeps within the limits. He cannot go over the bounds of the narrative (Greg. Nyss. *Vit Macr.* 20.5 Silvas/18 Maraval). Therefore, we only get direct speech from Macrina in small doses. This absence is heightened in the final day of Macrina's life: Gregory places some small selections of direct speech right before and right after the deathbed conversation (at Greg. Nyss. *Vit Macr.* 19.4 Silvas/17 Maraval and 21.1 Silvas/ 19 Maraval) but only *narrates* that key moment in indirect speech.

His concern with excess does not keep him from recording Macrina's long prayer at her death. Like Thecla, the predominant speech this philosophical woman is granted in the *biographical* text is a prayer addressed to God, which is not even meant to be overheard by others. Although Macrina is not alone with God, as Thecla was, Gregory emphasizes that she is concerned to talk only to God: she has turned away from the other people in her room, toward the east, to address her bridegroom directly. She ceases to dialogue with her brother and companions (ἀποστᾶσα τοῦ πρὸς ἡμᾶς διαλέγεσθαι, Greg. Nyss. *Vit. Macr.* 25.2 Silvas/23 Maraval) in order to conduct her conversation with God. Her words are hard to hear, which does not stop Gregory from being able to "accurately" reproduce them for his readers.

As Derek Krueger has explicated, Macrina's prayer echoes a eucharistic anaphora, complete with epiclesis (Krueger 2000). It is liturgical speech rather than philosophical speech. The rhythms are hymnic and repetitive rather than dialectic. Each rhythmic line contains citations of sacred scripture, woven together to make a biographical narrative. The biographical and the liturgical here blend into one.

In the *Life of Macrina*, Gregory depicts a female philosopher who lays claim to being wise through other sources of wisdom rather than traditional education. She expresses her wisdom verbally through liturgical modes of speaking like prayers. When Gregory scripts his wise sister into a philosophical dialogue, however, he is more comfortable having her display a range of traditional knowledge and a dialectic, rather than liturgical, mode of speech.

3.1.5 Conclusion

The *Life of Macrina* laid out the way of life of a new type of philosopher, without the advantages, or distractions, of traditional education. Macrina is able to achieve the goal of philosophy through her meditation, prayer, and singing. She ascended the heights and brought others with her. Sometimes this required downgrading the traditional education that those others had already received, as was the case with her brother Basil.

If the *Life of Macrina* wanted to reveal a philosopher, it frustrates anyone wishing to know the details of Macrina's philosophical commitments. Gregory tells us the topics upon which she discoursed at her death but does not tell us the steps of her argument or its ultimate conclusions. One might approach our next text, the dialogue *On the Soul and Resurrection*, with more hope. Here we are held out the possibility of hearing the very words spoken by the philosopher. If Socrates gained his credentials by being in dialogues rather than in biographies, we might think that this would be the easier place to see Macrina's philosophy in action.

But framing the question in this way does not align with Gregory's own conception of what it means to see a philosopher in action. He believes that Macrina's philosophy is shown just as clearly in the biographical text as a dialogic one. The "narrative mode" of philosophy and the "verbal mode" of philosophy are both valuable witnesses of the philosopher, even if they are unmixed. Gregory's Macrina, more than either of the other women in this Element, is just as strongly characterized as a philosopher in both genres in which she is commemorated.

3.2 *On the Soul and Resurrection:* A Philosopher in Dialogue

In *On the Soul and Resurrection* (= *De Anima*), Gregory activates Macrina's characterization as a philosopher and educator of his own disordered passions and ideas. Macrina's method in the beginning of the dialogue is to draw out the moral implications of logical arguments.

The first sentence spoken in direct discourse is Macrina's command inspired by a passage in 1 Thessalonians: "One ought not grieve for those who have fallen asleep, for this is the passion only of those who have no hope" (cf. 1 Thessalonians 4:13). Her opening salvo is a moral argument (*one ought not*) based on a logical argument echoed in the Sacred Scriptures. The opening displays a logical Macrina countering a Gregory made irrational through emotional turmoil. As Smith clarifies, Gregory's grief is caused by a mistake of judgment, not simply an excess of emotion (J. W. Smith 2004, 96–98), and Macrina's therapy is a therapy of logic.

3.2.1 *Women in Gregory's Model, Plato's* Phaedo

Some of the gendered aspects of this dialogue only come to the surface when we compare the text with Gregory's inspirational source text, Plato's *Phaedo*. The *Phaedo* could also be seen as the therapy of logic over the emotions caused by approaching death. But Plato is explicit about sending away the women from the scene because they are unable to train their emotions in the necessary way.

I would further argue that the difference between the two texts' treatment of women is due to the different relationships the women have with children and cycles of procreation.

When Phaedo first arrives in the prison on the day of Socrates' death, Socrates is not alone. His wife Xanthippe is with him, holding their young child. At the same moment that Socrates is released from his chains, Phaedo says that Xanthippe sits next to him holding their little child (ἔχουσάν τε τὸ παιδίον αὐτοῦ, Plato *Phaedo* 60a). She is unable to be released from the physical requirements of motherhood that hold her back from the philosophical ascent demonstrated by Socrates. She wails out a line of sorrow before Socrates asks that she be taken away.

Women reappear at the end of the *Phaedo* to perform a similar job. Once again, their lack of emotional self-control requires their removal. Primarily, they are there to serve as negative examples to the men: Socrates chides them by saying that inordinate weeping was the reason that he had sent away the women, so they better behave.

> "What is this," he said, "you strange fellows. It is mainly for this reason that I sent the women away, to avoid such unseemliness, for I am told one should die in good omened silence. So keep quiet and control yourselves."
>
> (Plato *Phaedo* 117d–e, trans. Grube)

> Ἐκεῖνος δέ, Οἷα, ἔφη, ποιεῖτε, ὦ θαυμάσιοι. ἐγὼ μέντοι οὐχ ἥκιστα τούτου ἕνεκα τὰς γυναῖκας ἀπέπεμψα, ἵνα μὴ τοιαῦτα πλημμελοῖεν· καὶ γὰρ ἀκήκοα ὅτι ἐν εὐφημίᾳ χρὴ τελευτᾶν. ἀλλ᾽ ἡσυχίαν τε ἄγετε καὶ καρτερεῖτε.

The men in Plato's dialogue manage to do what the women are deemed incapable of, control their emotions and continue the conversation until Socrates' death, up to when comely silence is required. The Platonic text makes the link between gender and emotional control explicit.[31]

Gregory's weeping is not unlike that of the male disciples of Socrates. But Gregory does not use the uncontrollable emotions of women as the shaming counterexample, as Socrates feels free to do. Macrina, in her Socrates function, shames Gregory into self-control without recourse to gendered arguments at all. Perhaps one of the main reasons that she is able to do so is that she is not holding physical children like Xanthippe and the other women in the *Phaedo*. She has

---

[31] Wilson-Kaster looks at this link with the *Phaedo*. Her point is to raise the difference between Socrates' response to Xanthippe and Macrina's response to Gregory (Wilson-Kaster 1979, 114). However, I think that this is not quite the correct parallel. Gregory's weeping is not only like Xanthippe but also like the male followers of Socrates. The gendered point is that Gregory is not told he is being unmanly by Macrina, as the male disciplines of Socrates are. They are both educated out of their overly emotional response, but gendered shame is not the method employed by Macrina as it is by Socrates.

broken her physical ties with the world. Just as, in the *Life of Macrina*, her mother was unable to join her in the life of philosophy until all of her children were taken care of, so too Macrina's lifelong virginity allows her to evade the burden of the physical connected *by necessity* to the women in Plato's *Phaedo*.

3.2.2 Macrina's Knowledge in On the Soul and Resurrection

Although, in the *Life*, Gregory narrates Macrina's education as being based on Christian texts alone, in the dialogue, she displays accurate knowledge of non-Christian philosophical schools of thought, such as Epicureanism and Platonism. She also displays a range of other types of knowledge traditionally part of the philosophical curriculum, such as astronomy and physics.

Elizabeth Clark points to this range of Macrina's knowledge to suggest that Macrina speaks in Gregory's voice rather than being a witness to educated women in late antiquity.

> Here she instructs her brother on the Epicurean denial of providence and espousal of atomistic theory; on humans as the microcosm of the universe; on the relation of the soul and body in the afterlife. She speaks of the love that draws us to the Good. She evinces knowledge of Aristotelian logic, and borrows analogies from contemporary astronomy and physics to score her points. Do not such accounts encourage us to believe that fourth-century Christian women could expound theological and philosophical wisdom as well as their male counterparts? Are these women not heroines who can be added to the pages of "her-story"? Not too readily, I would suggest: the "social logic" of the text has less to do with "real women" than with an elaboration of theological points that troubled their authors. (E. A. Clark 1998, 23–24)

I wholeheartedly agree that we must always remember that Gregory is the author of the dialogue, with his own specific theological agenda. Yet, Clark does not go on at length to discuss what theological points she believes were being elaborated and why they demanded a female mouthpiece. Macrina's knowledge is one of the key examples where genre interferes with the characterization of the same "character" across multiple works. Why did Gregory think it important to imbue his sister with this kind of knowledge in *On the Soul and Resurrection* and to deny it to his sister in the *Life of Macrina*?

The dialogue *On the Soul and Resurrection* is initiated with a crisis, when Gregory encounters his sister unexpectedly near death. It may seem that it is primarily a crisis of emotion, but Macrina quickly leads Gregory into making his misgivings verbal and ordered, in such a way that she can refute. She labels Gregory's first misgivings about why death causes sorrow as the opinion of those who are "rather unreasonable" (ἡ τῶν ἀλογωτέρων συνήθεια, Greg. Nyss.

De Anima Intro.1.7 Silvas). She labels his second misgivings, that there is no evidence that the soul survives death, as based on the wrong authorities, namely Epicureanism rather than the Scriptures. It is here that we first confront the question of Macrina's technical philosophical education. What does Macrina know about Epicureanism and, by extension, about the history of philosophy? How adept is she at debating her opinion against other schools of philosophy?

The gauntlet has been thrown down and the sides are drawn up for the debate. Gregory presents the strong argument against the soul's immortality by claiming that the concept of the immortality of the soul is a noble lie crafted to encourage moral living. He claims this argument comes from Greek philosophers, without giving that phrase a negative valence. Macrina is not impressed, but rather insults such ideas by calling them "external trifles."

> Gregory: ... And there are some among the Greek who have not a small reputation for philosophy, who think and say such things.
> Macrina: Who gives a fig for such external nonsense! With such drivel the inventor of falsehood makes erroneous opinions believable as a blow to the truth.
>
> (Greg. Nyss. *De Anima* 1.1.4–5 Silvas)

> G. ... Καὶ εἰσί γέ τινες παρὰ τοῖς Ἕλλησιν οὐ μικρὰν ἔχοντες ἐπὶ φιλοσοφίᾳ τὴν δόξαν, οἳ ταῦτα ᾠήθησάν τε καὶ ἀπεφήναντο. –
> Μ. Ἔα, φησί, τοὺς ἔξωθεν λήρους, ἐν οἷς ὁ τοῦ ψεύδους εὑρέτης ἐπὶ βλάβῃ τῆς ἀληθείας πιθανῶς τὰς ἠπατημένας ὑπολήψεις συντίθησιν·

Macrina rejects Gregory's reliance on external authorities and arguments. In the process she also seems to characterize philosophy itself as foreign to the Christian mode of argumentation. But this is a red herring. Macrina's rejection of certain philosophical sects – Stoicism, but especially Epicureanism – is made in a very philosophical and learned way. In particular, she summarizes the teaching of Epicurus by name, suitably describing it with the uncommon and vivid metaphor of life as a bubble (Greg. Nyss. *Vit. Macr.* 1.1.13 Silvas). Her argument against the materialism of the Epicureans is that it is *not intellectual enough*, and that those who hold it have a small soul unable to look beyond material things to their cause. Macrina, therefore, is shown to be conversant with the teachings of the philosophical schools of thought and able to defend her own sect against them. She behaves like one of Plutarch's students in the *Reply to Colotes*, learning the ropes about how to persuasively address criticisms from the other philosophical sects (in the Plutarchian context, Epicureanism as well).

Secondly, like her Theclean model before her, she also knows about ancient science, and uses that knowledge at the service of philosophical argument. Nor is it a passing acquaintance: this dialogue might be the richest of all the Nyssan texts in its frequency of scientific example and detail (Ramelli 2020, 3). Morwenna Ludlow has investigated Macrina's scientific knowledge in this dialogue, focusing on two passages in particular: an astronomical section and a metaphor based on the mechanics of a water-propelled machine (Ludlow 2009). I will examine these two in turn.

First, Macrina shows an extensive amount of technical knowledge about astronomy. Astronomy and cosmology were a standard part of Neoplatonic philosophical education. Porphyry wrote an introduction to Ptolemy's *Tetrabiblos*, on stars, which survives,[32] and the final book of Iamblichus' monumental educational curriculum was dedicated to astronomy (O'Meara 1990). Ludlow explains that Macrina's cosmology – and specifically her understanding that the moon shines with the light of the sun – would have been part of specifically Platonic systems of thought. Peripatetics and Stoics had a different concept of the nature of the moon's glow (Ludlow 2009, 476–77). Astronomy was not a line of teaching separate from philosophy but was a constituent part of it, which, she argues, "firmly situates Gregory's comments on the moon in a philosophical rather than in a scientific context" (Ludlow 2009, 477).

One detail in Macrina's astronomical metaphor deserves greater consideration for its rhetorical effect and purpose. Macrina begins her excursus on the moon by asserting that Gregory knows these things because he has been taught them earlier by his (male) teacher (Greg. Nyss. *De Anima* 1.2.10 Silvas). I take the suggestion here to be that Gregory's education included Neoplatonic astronomy. But then Macrina ends the example by saying that sight itself is the teacher, if guided by the reason inside of us (Greg. Nyss. *De Anima* 1.2.17). It seems that Gregory's education was useless not only because he fails to remember the details at important points but also because simple observation could get you there without education. While Gregory needed a teacher to show him this, an external teacher was not, strictly speaking, necessary.

There is a tension here in the characterization of Macrina. She is displayed as an expert, but it is unclear how or why she could have gained her astronomical expertise. Gregory wants to suggest that it might be due to direct observation and intellection, while also pointing to the fact that Macrina knows that Gregory learned this in school – implying that *she* learned it through overhearing, much like Monica will learn about the expectations of the genre of the philosophical

---

[32] Aaron Johnson provides a helpful introduction to Porphyry's commentary on Ptolemy's *Tetrabiblos* (Johnson 2013, 159–64).

dialogue in our next section presumably through overhearing male classroom discussions. This is one particularly salient example of the wider trend of the dialogue: Macrina repeatedly shows more knowledge of secular affairs in *On the Soul and Resurrection* than Gregory permitted her in the *Life of Macrina*.

There is a second example of Macrina's knowledge that sits at odds with Gregory's claim in the *Life of Macrina* that she was solely educated on sacred texts and subjects. Once Macrina tries to show that there must be a mind behind the world with her astronomical examples, Gregory suggests that perhaps the world is an automaton: it only looks like there is a mind, while in fact all motion actually has a purely mechanical cause. At first, it appears that Gregory is the expert on this. He chooses the example and gives a brief description of how such machines work. But it turns out that Macrina has something of Rosie the Riveter about her. She too is an expert in the way such machines function. She goes on at much greater length than Gregory about the means of constructing and manipulating such a machine. The point of her argument is that there must be a mind that created such a complex work (Greg. Nyss. *De Anima*, 2.28 Silvas) – a mind like her own that understands how it functions, having made it to suit a particular need.

One might argue that these are both just barely possible bits of knowledge for a woman without a secular education to have. Macrina must have observed the moon most nights of her life, especially since, as Gregory himself tells us, she was awake frequently in the night for prayer. And the mechanism might have been something that would be useful on a large farm of the type for which Macrina had responsibility. Yet, Macrina uses these examples *philosophically*, as does Gregory. At the very end of her description, she says that her foregoing technical examples have proven that there is an immaterial mind behind all things that appear in the world (Greg. Nyss. *De Anima* 2.35 Silvas).

3.3 Conclusion

We must ceaselessly recall that Macrina is always ventriloquized. Macrina has whatever knowledge Gregory wishes her to have. This does not have to be accurate, and, in line with Elizabeth Clark, we can suspect the attribution all we like. However, an important point is that Gregory wants to ascribe this kind of knowledge to his sister, and he has to maneuver delicately between his ascription of secular knowledge to her in *On the Soul and Resurrection* and his assertion in the biography that she did not have a secular education. When women are put into philosophical dialogues, the authors are pushed to show them speaking as philosophers traditionally would. The requirements of the different genres help explain the differences between Macrina's characterization in the biography and in the dialogue. In the *Life of Macrina*, Gregory depicts a female philosopher who lays claim to being wise through other sources of wisdom rather than traditional education, while in *On the Soul and Resurrection*, she clearly displays a range of traditional knowledge.

In both the dialogue and the biography, Macrina takes on the role of teacher to her male relatives. She is the ideal to which they aspire. Even those who should be her superiors (such as her mother) are her students. Scholars have primarily tried to place Macrina's educational status in relationship to Plato's *Symposium* where she is most often looked at as another Diotima (Burrus 2005). However, despite the temptation of placing her as a second Diotima because of gender alignment, it is much more accurate to say that Macrina is another Socrates (Wilson-Kaster 1979).[33] How does that in turn affect Gregory? Does he become a second Xanthippe, but one who is taught to successfully control his grief (suggested by Wilson-Kaster 1979, 114)? I think that the stronger textual parallels are between Gregory and Socrates' *male* disciples in Plato's *Phaedo*, who are able to turn from uncontrolled mourning to rational conversation. However, a revaluation of the female is also present. Gregory is not shamed into controlling his emotions in contrast with women, as Socrates' disciples were in the *Phaedo*, but in *emulation* of a woman. There is a fundamental unity of virtue regardless of gender, and Gregory can learn through watching and imitating a woman and her exceptional self-control.

Telling the story only in relationship to Plato's gendered dynamics overlooks the other female teachers and philosophers that came between.[34] The most salient for Macrina is Thecla.[35] In particular, Methodius' Thecla had already paved the way for the development of a female dialogic philosopher. But while Thecla's influence was mainly in imaginative female circles, with Macrina, Gregory moves into the more radical position of creating a philosophical woman who served as a model to men, including, most especially, himself.

---

[33] Burrus broadens her interpretation in a later analysis. "Similarly, in the literary doublet to this work, Gregory's dialogue *On the Soul and Resurrection*, Gregory can play the weeping virgin to Macrina's Socrates or Socrates to her Diotima" (Burrus 2007, 76; cf. 2000, 112).

[34] Virginia Burrus mentions Methodius' Thecla as an intervening dialogic woman between Plato's Diotima and Gregory's Macrina, but still manages to push her aside quickly in order to focus on a Plato–Gregory pairing (Burrus 2000, 112–13).

[35] The notable exception to this is the illuminating article by Patricia Wilson-Kaster, which has not had the impact in the scholarly discussion on the Macrina literature that it deserves (Wilson-Kaster 1979).

4 Monica, Who "Grasped the Very Citadel of Philosophy" (Aug. *De Beat. Vit.* 2.10)

Monica's role in Augustine's life is well known through his presentation of her as a guiding force in his conversion in his *Confessions*, especially in his eulogy of her when she dies in *Confessions* Book 9.8–13.[36] But about ten years before he wrote the *Confessions*,[37] he had already scripted his mother as a lover of wisdom in his dialogues. Monica plays a role in three of Augustine's Cassiciacum dialogues: speaking roles in the *De Ordine* and the *De Beata Vita*, and a non-speaking part in the *Contra Academicos*.

Despite Augustine's designation of his mother as such, some scholars have found it hard to accept Monica's credentials as a philosopher.[38] While it is true that Monica did not have access to the level of education that she sacrificed so much so that her son could achieve, Augustine's assertion that she is still truly a philosopher is part of his reorientation of the definition of philosophy into new territory, territory that was not tied to educational level or dialectical know-how. This terminological shift is strongest in the dialogues, becoming less important to Augustine by the time he writes the *Confessions*.

To continue the parallels with the previous sections, I will first look at Augustine's portrayal of his mother as a philosopher in a biographical mode in his *Confessions*. Then I will turn to his portrayal of her in his early dialogues. This will reverse the chronological compositions of these works, in distinction to the other two examples, where the biographical version chronologically preceded the dialogical.

This flipping is not accidental. As his valuation of philosophy shifted, so too did his genre,[39] and also the level of explicitness with which he characterizes his mother as a philosopher. Even though Augustine connects his mother with the life of philosophy in the dialogues, the dialogic Monica already pushes against the traditions of the philosophical dialogues. Augustine's portrayal of Monica in dialogic mode is much closer to her portrayal in narrative mode in the *Confessions* than the characterizations of Thecla or Macrina across the works that feature them. In particular, there is no discrepancy between her purported

---

[36] There is a preference among many scholars to spell Monica's name with two ens since it appears this way in the oldest manuscripts of the *Confessions*, the only place where Monica's name appears in Augustine's corpus. However, I have opted for the more common Monica in this Element. Gillian Clark has helpfully summarized the debate about Monica's Berber heritage and its impact on the spelling of her name (G. Clark 2015, 126–28).

[37] The dialogues were written in 386 and the *Confessions* in 397 CE.

[38] E.g. Vaught says in passing, "Monica is not a philosopher" (Vaught 2004, 130).

[39] Gillian Clark has argued that although Augustine leaves behind the philosophical dialogue as a genre, he does so because his role has changed to a bishop, not because he saw it as a necessary concomitant of his Christian convictions (G. Clark 2008).

lack of traditional education in the *Confessions* and her performance as a philosopher in the dialogues. Even in the dialogues, her wisdom is not ascribed to traditional education, but instead has its source from her life in the church. When she quotes sources, they are biblical passages or lines from contemporary hymns written by Ambrose rather than allusions to Plato or the Stoics. Her greatest philosophical skill is breaking down Augustine's pretensions as a skeptical teacher and providing solutions at impasses in the argument through her knowledge of the Christian life of the living church. We observe Augustine managing to incorporate those who are not hypereducated into his definition of the philosophical life. And since Monica's verbal contributions in the dialogues are less extensive than those of Thecla in Methodius' *Symposium* or Macrina in Gregory's *On the Soul and Resurrection*, the difference in the length of the speeches attributed to Monica in the two modes is less distinct.

Also in distinction from the preceding examples, the biographical work is not a work focused on the female philosopher but one in which she plays a supporting role. Augustine did not write a *Life of Monica*; he wrote a *Confessions* (G. Clark 2015, 8). There is not even a synopsis of Monica and Patricius in Book 1, like we have for Macrina's mother at the beginning of the *Life of Macrina* (2.2 Silvas). While Augustine's narrative of his own life is chronological, he chooses a different mode for his "biography" of his mother.[40] Monica's richest treatment in the *Confessions*, and the only place where we glimpse her childhood, is embedded in the story of her death, in the final narrative book of the *Confessions*, Book 9. The sandwiching of Monica's story by her death allows Augustine to end with his liturgical request for his readers to pray for his mother. In addition, Augustine uses this narrative arrangement to argue that Monica has achieved the detachment from earthly concerns that typify a philosopher, which can be observed most vibrantly at the moment of death (E. Clark 1999, 18).

4.1 Monica in Augustine's *Confessions*

Monica at first glance seems incommensurate with the other two women looked at in this Element. She came from a different part of the Empire, spoke a different language, and was never the central character in any of her texts. Yet there are important moments of contact between the narrative of Monica in the *Confessions* and those of Thecla and Macrina. With Macrina, Monica's presentation as a philosopher shares a focus on death, which encompasses her

---

[40] In some compelling ways, Monica's mini-biography is parallel to Alypius' "biography" found in *Conf.* 6.7.11–6.8.16 (noted by Courcelle, cited at O'Donnell 1992, 115). However, the framing of the analeptic moment with Monica's death affects the interpretation of her story in ways that are not found in the Alypius narrative.

narratives in important ways. And with Thecla, Monica's narrative shares a central moment at a window, where they are both allowed to withdraw from the mundane ties that bind them to a particular way of life and touch an alternative. I will treat these two in turn after discussing Augustine's story of Monica's "education."

4.1.1 Monica's Education in the Confessions

Monica is present throughout the *Confessions*, but her biography is concentrated in Book 9, at the moment of her death. Augustine begins with a simple statement that his mother died –"mater defuncta est" (Aug. *Conf.* 9.8.17) – before analeptically flashing back to her childhood and married life.

Augustine plays with the idea, made famous in Thucydides' rendition of Pericles' Funeral Oration (Thucydides *Peloponnesian War* 2.45), that a respectable woman's life should be passed over in silence, and rejects it (Aug. *Conf.* 9.8.18). He declares that he will not pass over (*non praeteribo*) whatever his soul births (*parturit*) about God's little serving girl (*famula*). Augustine figures himself as pregnant with words, tapping into a long history of metaphorically pregnant males,[41] but also priming us for a discussion that focuses not merely on Monica's physical motherhood but also on her spiritual pregnancy. Monica gave birth to Augustine twice over, he claims, both in body (*carne*) and in spirit (*corde*). From his own dual birth, he smoothly moves to talking about Monica's birth, parentage, and education.

> I will speak not about her gifts, but about your gifts in her, nor that she made or educated herself. (Aug. *Conf.* 9.8.17)[42]
>
> non eius sed tua dicam dona in eam, neque enim se ipsa fecerat aut educaverat se ipsam.

As Augustine tells it, Monica was educated neither by herself nor by her parents. Instead, the "rod of Christ" educated her in the fear of the Lord (*et erudivit eam in timore tuo virga Christi tui*), which Proverbs 9:10 claims is the beginning of wisdom. Augustine goes through the two-step process of this education, whose lessons are self-control and docility rather than the liberal arts. Monica is first educated by a slave woman. But this lesson does not fully form Monica's habits. She only learns self-control when she is shamed by the statement of an unworthy teacher – an angry slave woman.

---

[41] See Leitao for the deep history of this image and LaValle Norman for an early Christian use (Leitao 2012; LaValle Norman 2019a).

[42] All translations from Augustine's *Confessions* are my own.

Augustine's story of Monica's childhood education reveals a network of female teachers. As a child, Monica is put under the charge of a Christian female household slave (*famulae … decrepitae*) rather than her biological mother (*nec disciplinam diligentiam matris*). Augustine had introduced Monica herself as a *famula*, or serving girl, when he first mentioned her in this passage (Aug. *Conf.* 9.8.18), which creates a further link between Monica and her slave educator. The old *famula* taught Monica how to be a *famula* herself, even though she was a freeborn girl of some standing.

> Wherefore she undertook with diligence the care of her master's daughters and was occupied in vehemently correcting them with holy severity, if it was necessary, and in teaching them with sober prudence. (Aug. *Conf.* 9.8.17)

> unde etiam curam dominicarum filiarum conmissam diligentur gerebat, et erat in eis coercendis, cum opus esset, sancta severitate vehemens, atque in docendis sobria prudentia.

This trusted slave acts as a female pedagogue not only to Monica but to all the female children of her master (*dominicarum filiarum*). Her educative method is focused not on literate education, but instead on the acquisition of virtue. Later, Augustine will call her wise (*sagax anus*, Aug. *Conf.* 9.8.18).

However, the legacy of this unnamed female servile teacher is mixed. She fails in her primary goal of teaching Monica self-control. Monica starts to sneak straight wine from the storeroom (Aug. *Conf.* 9.8.18). Instead of the wise female slave, it is a different slave that shakes Monica of her habit, a slave in no way depicted as virtuous. Augustine draws the moral that it is God who teaches, using imperfect means to achieve the necessary education. Just as Augustine's own education by corporal punishment was not ideal for instilling in him a love of truth, yet nevertheless his learning was fundamental for God's purpose in his life (Aug. *Conf.* 1.12.19), so too, Monica's education comes via imperfect teachers like the spiteful slave women rather than through expected channels like the wise slave woman.

Augustine considers this story sufficient for telling us about Monica's education. This was the way that she was educated – in prudence and sobriety (*educata itaque pudice ac sobrie*, Aug. *Conf.* 9.9.19). Equipped with this moral, rather than literate, education from a line of female teachers, both good and bad, Monica then goes on to become a teacher herself.

First, it seems that she will be a teacher of her husband Patricius, as the story moves to tell of how she navigated her complex marriage. But while all the initial signs point to Monica being Patricius' teacher, leading ultimately to his embrace of Christianity before death, Augustine avoids using any terminology of education for her influence on her husband. Instead of saying that Monica taught her husband, Augustine instead redirects her educational energies to other wives in Thagaste. Monica teaches these women her syllabus (*docebat illa institutum suum*, Aug. *Conf.* 9.9.20); namely, how to avoid physical domestic abuse through docility. Monica maintains the female line of teachers in an explicit way, schooling other women in the wisdom she has gained directly from God and with the help of the *sagax anus*.

The narration of Monica's education ends with the summary statement:

> Such was the woman, with you being her internal teacher in the school of her heart. (Aug. *Conf.* 9.9.21)

> qualis illa erat docente te magistro intimo in schola pectoris.

O'Donnell connects these last summative words about Monica's education with the authority Augustine gives her in the Cassiciacum dialogues: "authority is hers, for she has been to a better school, and had a better teacher, than Augustine himself," noting that the word "teacher" is applied to God alone after Book 6 of the *Confessions* (O'Donnell 1992, 120). What was intimated by the transfer of teaching from the good slave to the bad slave in the earlier story is here made explicit. God is Monica's teacher. Although she had a good teacher in the wise slave woman, the means that God uses are the negative ones: the sassy slave and a violent husband. Although Augustine chooses to use terminology of education when going through his mother's early years, it is an education displaced from an earthly school to a heavenly school.

4.1.2 Monica and the "Vision/Audition/Imbibition at Ostia"

After this excursus on Monica's education and subsequent teaching career among the women of Thagaste, Augustine returns to the days before her death. A conversation that took place at the port town of Ostia is perhaps the most famous moment in Monica's life, because of the important position it takes in Augustine's narration of his own. Like Thecla in her *Acts*, the decisive moment takes place at a window. And like the women in Methodius' *Symposium*, there is a garden, which puts them in touch with the original beatitude of Eden (*incumbentes ad quandam fenestram unde hortus intra domum quae nos habebat prospectabatur*, Aug. *Conf.* 9.10.23). But while Thecla was listening in on others' speech, Monica and Augustine are making it, discussing (*conloquebamur*) sweetly, until they can no longer see what is before them. James O'Donnell has influentially remarked that this event would be better called the "Audition at Ostia" rather than the "Vision at Ostia" (O'Donnell 1992, 133), which is a helpful correction. However, it in turn obscures the interweaving of hearing and seeing that pervades the scene.[43] The mother and son move beyond their eyes and ears. The garden that was visible to Monica and Augustine drops away as they enter into their own minds, guided by the invisible assistance of God (*occultis tuis modis*, Aug. *Conf.* 9.10.23), rather than any physical sense. Instead, Augustine says that they gulp with the mouth of the heart the heavenly rivers of God's fountain of life (*sed inhiabamus ore cordis in superna fluenta fontis tui, fontis vitae, qui est apud te*, Aug. *Conf.* 9.10.23). Perhaps, then, it might best be called the "Imbibition of Ostia."

The "Vision at Ostia" has become a touchstone for many arguments about mystical experience, the use of dialogue and mutual support to get there, and whether or not it is necessary to remove oneself from the physical world to achieve spiritual insight. But the question for us is what this recollected event has to do with philosophy.

In the opening of this Element, we discussed the important recurring image of the mountain, upon which dwelt a desirable, allegorical woman. The mystical experience at Ostia participates in this broad narrative. The verticality of their mental ascent is emphasized (*adhuc ascendebamus*, Aug. *Conf.* 9.10.24), and at the top of their ascent is a green field, rich with pasture.[44] There they find Wisdom. The mountain-top garden of Arete in Methodius is not far off. But it is not only the male Augustine who rises up to touch the desired woman – Monica herself joins in the quest. As in Methodius' scene-setting, the gendering of the questers as feminine modifies the allegory of eroticized ascent.[45]

Eternal Wisdom (*aeternam sapientiam*), rather than being allegorized as a desirable woman here, takes on an unexpected male coloring despite her grammatically feminine gender. Monica and Augustine are both able to "touch" her with an impulse of the heart before falling back,[46] but the true goal of life, according to Augustine, is to remain in perpetual contact with her.

---

[43] For example, there is a return to terminology of sight at the very end of *Conf.* 9.10.25. The first half of this paragraph is full of the world falling silent, with repeated terminology of sounds and their cessation. But at the end, Augustine turns to vision: "If this were sustained and other visions of a very different kind were withdrawn, and this one vision should ravish and absorb and enclose its beholder in interior joy, so that life might be always thus, like that moment of perception, for which we sighed ... " (*si continuetur hoc et subtrahantur aliae visiones longe imparis generis et haec una rapiat et absorbeat et recondat in interiora gaudia spectatorem suum, ut talis sit sempiterna vita, quale fuit hoc momentum intellegentiae, cui suspiravimus ...*).

[44] " ... and so we touched a place of unfailing richness, where You pasture Israel forever with true pasturage" (... *ut attingeremus regionem ubertatis indeficientis, ubi pascis Israhel in aeternum veritate pabulo*), Aug. *Conf.* 9.10.24.

[45] In this, Anne-Marie Bowery's assertion that "their shared mystical experience represents the sexless universality of experience" comes close to the mark insofar as both feminine and masculine metaphors are applied in the text to humans of both genders, but the experience does not seem accurately described as "sexless" (Bowery 2007, 77).

[46] This "touching" is mentioned twice: *attingimus eam modice toto ictu cordis* (Aug. *Conf.* 9.10.24) and *rapida cogitatione attingimus* (Aug. *Conf.* 9.10.25).

Augustine speaks of this perpetual contact not in terms of conquest but rather of being conquered, making the wise pursuer of wisdom into the passive member of the erotic relationship, wanting the vision to "ravish and absorb and enclose its beholder in interior joy, so that life might be always thus" (*et haec una rapiat et absorbeat et recondat in interiora gaudia spectatorem suum, ut talis sit sempiterna vita*, Aug. *Conf.* 9.10.25). Seeing becomes not an active invasion but rather a point of contact where the beholder is ravished by the vision rather than the other way around.

He and his mother were joined in this moment, both sighing for that union in which they were the passive partners. Augustine joins his mother in a moment described in feminized language. And in so doing, he likewise joins in Methodius of Olympus' inversion of the mountain-top encounter with an allegorical female, similarly feminizing the quester. Monica's presence alongside her son makes the feminization more obvious and also more naturalized in the context.

In the "Vision at Ostia," what is emphasized most is that wisdom does not exist in the past or the future but is forever in the present. All things become through her, but she does not become. The repetition and alteration of tenses of "to be" (*esse*) and "to become" (*fieri*) make these lines into a nearly trance-inducing incantation, inviting the reader to share in the mystical vision (Aug. *Conf.* 9.10.24). The reader is invited to join Monica's lead with Augustine's fellowship, and imaginatively "become female" for a moment of philosophical fulfillment, imagined as being ravished by wisdom, sighing at the momentary nature of the embrace, and longing for it to be made permanent in the future.

4.1.3 Monica's Death in the Confessions

If Monica and Augustine's garden-topped ascent reminds us of Thecla and her companions in Methodius' *Symposium*, then when Augustine finally ends his Monica section with her deathbed, surrounded by male relatives (Aug. *Conf.* 9.11.28), we are in the world familiar from Gregory of Nyssa's two writings about his sister Macrina examined above.

Monica struggles to be understood with the growing pain. Her discussion is not a long philosophical dialogue as she dies but instead a short plea linked to the sacraments. As we will also see in the Cassiciacum dialogues, Augustine links Monica's wisdom with the life of the Church. Her dying dialogue is a request for her two sons to remember her at mass, wherever they may be (*tantum illud vos rogo, ut ad domini altare memineritis mei, ubiubi fueritis*, Aug. *Conf.* 9.11.27, with repeated references at 9.13.36 and 9.13.37). Her perspective has completely changed from her earlier desire to be buried in her homeland. Now she longs for the pastures of eternal wisdom which she will soon enter. Her true home is elevated rather than buried.

There is wailing, pain, and sadness. Then someone starts to sing, bringing order to disorder. The movement from death to lamentation to the order of the Psalms is richly parallel with that in Gregory of Nyssa's *Life of Macrina* (28.4 Silvas/26 Maraval). At Monica's funeral, there are groups of men and women who join in the singing of the Psalms (*multi fratres ac religiosae feminae*, Aug. *Conf.* 9.12.31). But the antiphonal Psalm-singing is not enough for Augustine. He is only freed from his grief when the words of an Ambrosian song come to mind (Aug. *Conf.* 9.12.32). He weeps and is calmed. We will see in the next section Monica also relying on the poetic words of Ambrose at a key moment in the Cassiciacum dialogues. Augustine tells us that the song recalls in particular the *conversation* that Monica had shared with Augustine (*ancillam tuam conversationemque eius piam in te*, Aug. *Conf.* 9.12.33). We are close to the world of the dialogues which we will be turning to next. Monica and Augustine, then, both had the same Ambrosian poetic texts memorized, and Augustine seems to associate them in particular with his mother.

The last words of his mother requesting liturgical prayers are so central to him that he returns to them at the very end of the Monica section in Book 9, addressing his readers. He asks that all who are reading this remember Monica and Patricius at mass (Aug. *Conf.* 9.13.37). This is the only time that Augustine mentions his parents' names. The fellow Christians are his brothers, sons of God and with the Catholic church as mother (*et fratrum meorum sub te patre in matre catholica*, Aug. *Conf.* 9.13.37). But one mother does not supplant the other (Sehorn 2015). Augustine admits that it is the church that is the true mother, but also asks his readers to remember his mother in the flesh.

4.1.4 Monica at Cassiciacum in the Confessions

I have focused mainly on the end of Book 9 of the *Confessions*, from the moment when Augustine tells us that Monica died to the flashbacks he narrates about her earlier life. But Monica has appeared a bit earlier in Book 9 when Augustine speaks about his time on vacation in a villa in Cassiciacum, leading up to his baptism in Milan (Aug. *Conf.* 9.4.7–9.4.12).

> What words I gave to you, my God, when I read the Psalms of David, faithful songs, sounds of piety that blocked out the pompous spirit, unskilled in our twinned love of you, a catechumen vacationing in a villa with a catechumen, Alypius, with our mother joined to us, who had the outward shape of a woman, a manly faith, an old woman's security, a motherly love and a Christian piety. What words I was giving to you in those Psalms ... (Aug. *Conf.* 9.4.8)

quas tibi, deus meus, voces dedi, cum legerem psalmos David, cantica fidelia, sonos pietatis excludentes turgidum spiritum, rudis in germano amore tuo, catechumenus in villa cum catechumeno Alypio feriatus, matre adhaerente nobis muliebri habitu, virili fide, anili securitate, materna caritate, christiana pietate! quas tibi voces dabam in psalmis illis . . .

First, Augustine speaks of a twinned love that he shares with Alypius, but then adds in a third person to the two: Monica. Augustine gives Monica's description in an extended ablative absolute organized around pairs. The first pair connects across gender – Monica has the aspect of a woman but the faith of a man. The second pair connects across stages in a woman's life – Monica has the benefits of old age while still being a mother. Finally, Augustine adds one more description that is not paired at all, but absolute – Christian piety. None of these adulatory descriptors are concerned with the intellectual or philosophical life.

Augustine squeezes his description of Monica between repeated clauses about the Psalms. He circles back, repeating the same phrase that he began the section with, having picked up Alypius and Monica on the way. The Psalms will continue to be associated with Monica throughout Book 9. As we saw at the very end of the book, the reading of the Psalms at her funeral pulls the mourners out of their grief, even if for Augustine it is Ambrose's hymn that is most effective. Monica is connected with book-learning, but the book is the Psalms rather than books of secular learning.

When Augustine speaks about the composition of the dialogues during this time, he describes them as debates with his companions (*libri disputati cum praesentibus*, Aug. *Conf.* 9.4.7). He also mentions that Alypius wished him to make fundamental changes – in particular, to remove all explicit references to Christ. Augustine does not choose, however, to rehash the *content* of the dialogues in the *Confessions*, or even to mention the topics that they discussed and about which he wrote. Looking back, he does not focus on his teaching young boys or discussing the progression of the liberal arts. Instead of philosophical questions pursued in those debates, he focuses on other activities he carried out during this vacation at Cassiciacum: reading the Psalms and learning to pray to God.

4.1.5 Conclusion

Throughout his narrative of his mother in Book 9, Augustine avoids calling Monica a philosopher. He emphasizes that she was educated and was able to educate others in the "rod of discipline." She demonstrated the wisdom she had gained by being able to die well, with detachment from physical concerns. And, perhaps most centrally, she was linked with Augustine as they did the typical thing which philosophers do, namely, ascend the heights and encounter an allegorical woman, tying her tightly into the ambit of images of the life of philosophy. But only in the Cassiciacum dialogues themselves is she associated explicitly with philosophical terminology.

Augustine's rereading of Cassiciacum that he gives in the *Confessions* fits with the different presentation of Monica across the two texts. The Monica of the *Confessions* is not explicitly named a philosopher in much the same way that the report of the philosophical dialogues he wrote at the time are compacted in favor of recollections of prayer and healings. Such a shift reminds us that we need to take genre seriously when we compare how different texts by the same author differ in their treatment of characters and topics. When Gillian Clark talks about how the dialogues and the *Confessions* treat Monica differently, she focuses on the difference in time rather than the difference in genre (G. Clark 2015, 16). But the difference in time has led Augustine to a new choice of genre, to a narrative genre which is more open to presenting a woman as a wise teacher without labeling her a philosopher. In the dialogues, on the other hand, Augustine does not hesitate to associate his mother directly not only with wisdom but with philosophy itself.

4.2 Monica in Augustine's Cassiciacum Dialogues

Compared with other ancient philosophical dialogues, the characters in Augustine's dialogues form a motley crew, mostly because they show a huge discrepancy of experience and ability. Augustine is the clever and educated teacher, surrounded by students, uneducated relatives, and educated friends.[47] Augustine uses the setting and the writing of the dialogues to think through the necessity of a secular education for the new life upon which he is about to embark with his baptism in the coming months. Into these narratives, Augustine weaves his mother, popping in and out, sometimes sitting with his students, sometimes busy with meal preparations, as part of his larger concerns about education and the Christian life.

Augustine includes Monica's words in two of his works written during this time: the *De Ordine* and the *De Beata Vita*. She also makes a minor appearance in *Contra Academicos*, where she once calls the speakers to lunch, but does not participate in the conversation, an incident to which I will return in the conclusion to this section.

Catherine Conybeare contrasts Monica's presentation in Augustine's dialogues with the other women in this Element, Methodius' virgins and Gregory's Macrina, and concludes the following:

---

[47] Conybeare reminds us that Monica is not only present to represent the uneducated response. There are participants with even less education and intelligence than her (Conybeare 2006, 71).

Monnica is a far more rounded figure; she is properly integrated into the lifelike, and lively, scenarios of these dialogues. She, and her contributions, cannot be simply hived off as "symbolic". (Conybeare 2006, 66–67)

I would respond, however, that all three are "written women": Augustine uses Monica's unlettered insight to emphasize his changing understanding of how one accesses wisdom. Even if not abstracted to the level of a symbol, the character of Monica is used to achieve certain effects in male-authored texts.

4.2.1 Monica the Philosopher in Augustine's De Beata Vita

In the opening of his *De Beata Vita*, Augustine provides a cast list. His mother is listed first:

> For I am not ashamed to make known to your unique benevolence their names: first of all our mother, through whose merits I owe my entire life; Navigius my brother ... (Aug. *De Beat. Vit.* 1.6)[48]

> non enim vereor eos singulari benignitati tuae notos interim nominibus facere, in primis nostra mater, cuius meriti credo esse omne quod vivo; Navigius frater meus ...

Monica is the only woman in the list and the only one *not* given a proper name. As mentioned in the last section, Augustine names Monica only once in his entire corpus, in a moment when he pleads for prayers on her behalf at the end of Book 9 of the *Confessions* (Aug. *Conf.* 9.13.37). Here the lack of naming is particularly pointed because it is in a context of naming names. Augustine also includes in his cast list by name some of his relatives who have received no grammatical training at all, but whom nevertheless he would like to include. He makes no such excuse for Monica's education, either because she *had* received such an education or because it would not be so worthwhile to mention if she had not. At one interesting moment, Augustine asks Monica nonverbally to speak up on behalf of those who are less well educated, which she is unembarrassed to do (Aug. *De Beat. Vit.* 2.16).

Monica contributes to the three-day discussion of the *De Beata Vita* at multiple points, and her contributions vary from responding to Augustine's questions (3.22), asking her own questions (4.27), requesting clarification (2.16, 3.19), closing the conversation with a joke (1.16), and even singing (4.35). In all of these, she wins praise from her son and appears to be an ideal banqueter at this symposium of words: not only can she add to the intellectual content of the

---

[48] All translations from Augustine's *De Beata Vita* are my own.

conversation but she also correctly understands how to keep the right mood for the occasion.[49]

Conybeare is surely right to comment that "the *De Beata Vita* seems like Monnica's dialogue" (Conybeare 2006, 64). Conybeare argues that Augustine uses the figure of Monica to dramatize his own liminal status as he transforms from philosophical teacher into Christian leader. In the *De Beata Vita* in particular, Monica provides the means for Augustine to question the necessity to separate the soul from the body for philosophical ascent (Conybeare 2006, 88).

Yet she is not a representation of the body in distinction from the mind, but the union of them. Her contributions are intellectual. At the beginning of the second book of *De Ordine*,[50] Augustine claims that the contributions that Monica made during the course of the discussions recorded in *De Beata Vita* had convinced him to include her in all his subsequent dialogues because of "her talent and her mind burning for things divine" (*ingenium atque in res diuinas inflammatum animum*, Aug. *De Ordine* 2.1.1). At a moment emphasized in the narrative, she even anticipates Augustine's next comment. She does so from her own talent, rather than from the education that was the source for Augustine. Augustine claims that her unintended echoing of Cicero's *Hortensius* shows how she has achieved the ends of philosophy even without any access to a philosophical education ("Straightaway, mother, you have grasped the very citadel of philosophy," *Ipsam, inquam, prorsus, mater, arcem philosophiae tenuisti*, Aug. *De Beat. Vit.* 2.10).

Augustine presents Monica as a new type of ideal at odds with his former way of life, displaying a new mode of attaining knowledge without the preparation of the liberal arts.[51] In addition to being an example of piety, her status as a woman taps into the long-established connection between women and the material, and allows Augustine to move toward integrating the importance of embodiment in his recently embraced Christianity. Through the example of his mother, Augustine undercuts and overturns his own intellectualism, which he is struggling to leave behind. And while Monica is not the least educated among those present in these dialogues, and it would be too facile to see her as *simply*

---

[49] *De Beata Vita* takes place on Augustine's birthday, and while it is an intellectual feast rather than a physical feast that he primarily provides, his mother's presence reminds us of his physical birth as well.

[50] Conybeare suggests that this may have been due to a chilly or puzzled reception of Monica's role in Book 1 of the *De Ordine* by its dedicatee, Zenobius (Conybeare 2006: 110).

[51] In this vein, Elizabeth Clark insists on looking at the "Monica-function" rather than at "Monica," to see how Monica, as a character, fits into Augustine's larger theological projects. One of her conclusions is that Monica provides Augustine "with an alternative model of piety to that of educated men" (E. Clark 1999, 17).

a representative of non-educated Christian piety, nevertheless, she does manage to get to the heart of the issue without having been educated to the extent of Augustine's students or, of course, Augustine himself.

4.2.2 Monica the Philosopher in Augustine's De Ordine *and the Problem of* Feminae Philosophatae

The *De Ordine* is a dialogue about the order present in the universe. It begins cinematically as a nighttime conversation between Augustine and his students, trying to determine the cause of noises in the dark. It ends with a lengthy monologue in praise of the liberal arts. Monica's entrance into the conversation offers Augustine a moment to comment on whether women can do philosophy.

Monica is the most knowing of the female characters in ancient dialogues about the fact that she is an unusual choice of character in the genre.

> And meanwhile my mother came in and asked us how far we had gotten, for the topic under investigation was known to her too. When I had commanded that her entrance and her question be written down, as was our custom, she said, "What are you doing? For have I ever heard of women introduced in this type of discussion in those books which you all read?" (Aug. *De Ord.* 1.11.31)[52]

> atque interea mater ingressa est quaesiuitque a nobis, quid promovisse-mus; nam et ei quaestio nota erat. Cuius et ingressum et rogationem cum scribi nostro more iussissem. "quid agitis?" inquit; "numquidnam in illis quos legitis libris etiam feminas umquam audiui in hoc genus disputatio-nis inductas?"

The fact that Monica knows enough about philosophical dialogues to object to her own presence implies a secular education. And yet Monica calls those dialogues books that *they* read, not that *she* reads. If she is characterized as educated in secular learning here, it is from overhearing rather than being a regular participant in traditional education. She seems to be walking a line similar to Macrina in *On the Soul and Resurrection*, who reminds Gregory of what he learned previously from his male teachers (Greg. Nyss. *De Anima* 2.10; see Section 3.2 of this Element). But is Monica's assertion that she does not belong in the genre of the philosophical dialogue also an assertion that she does not belong within the group of philosophers?

Although Monica thinks that including a woman's voice is completely unheard of, Augustine knows that wise women have been consulted before in men's pursuit of wisdom. But his reference to an earlier tradition is opaque, and scholars argue over the sources to which he is pointing.

---

[52] All translations from Augustine's *De Ordine* are my own.

> For there were also women philosophers among the ancients, and your philosophy pleases me greatly. (Aug. *De Ord.* 1.11.31)

> Nam et feminae sunt apud veteres philosophatae et philosophia tua mihi plurimum placet.

James O'Donnell suggests that this is a reference to part of Cicero's *Hortensius*, which we know was so central in Augustine's conversion (O'Donnell 1992, 123). One of the fragments of the lost Ciceronian dialogue cites the speaker's mother (but not grandmother) as a source of wisdom.

> My grandmother used to say what you are saying, that all things happen by fate. But my mother, a wise woman, did not think so.
> (Maximus Taurinus, *Tractatus Contra Paganos*, PL 57.783A)

> Avia mea dicebat hoc, quod dicis, fato omnia fieri, mater autem, mulier sapiens, non existimavit.

I do not find it fully convincing that this is a reference to Cicero's lost dialogue because the evidence is so slight, but also because the *Hortensius* shows only one wise woman (*mulier sapiens*) rather than multiple female philosophers (*feminae … philosophatae*), referencing other *erroneous* women, like the speaker's grandmother. We have no indication of who spoke this line in the *Hortensius*, or whether it was elaborated within a longer analysis of wise women. What I find interesting, however, is that Augustine feels compelled to cite a precedent for his inclusion of the female voice, even if it leaves modern scholars in confusion about his sources. Augustine asserts the existence of a line of female philosophers in which he proudly places his own mother.

Monica as a female philosopher is the glue between the hinges of the first and second books of *De Ordine*. The first book is drawn to a close after Augustine's assertion of Monica's status as philosopher and her precedents in history. Yet his assertion here does not bring him to start a dialogue with his mother. Instead, her entrance and his speech put an end to the day's discussion (Aug. *De Ord.* 1.11.32).

When Book 2 opens, Augustine emphasizes his mother's philosophical abilities by pointing to her substantial contributions in *De Beata Vita*. It is her talent and religious devotion that bring her to the truth (*ingenium atque in res divinas inflammatum animum*, Aug. *De Ord.* 2.1.1). This twinned quality of Monica shines forth in Augustine's praise for her across the hinge between the two books of the *De Ordine*. Especially at the end of Book 1, Augustine praises Monica's true philosophy as distinct from the philosophy of this world (*philosophos huius mundi*, Aug. *De Ord.* 1.11.32), redefining "philosophy" to avoid the negative language about it found in Colossians 2:8. Monica's true philosophy is defined by love and lack of fear – neither of which seem dependent on rational ability.

However, at the beginning of Book 2, Augustine focuses specifically on Monica's mental abilities, her *mind* that is suited to true philosophy (*tanta mihi mens eius apparuerat, ut nihil aptius verae philosophiae videretur*, Aug. *De Ord.* 2.1.1). He decides to include her in all of his philosophical conversations because she is an able interlocutor, which she has shown in her earlier performance. Augustine does not fully resolve the tension at the heart of his understanding of Monica's philosophy, and whether it has more to do with love or with intellect.

4.2.3 Monica's Two Lunches and Two Songs

Monica's characterization occurs across multiple works, and in this way, her construction as a philosopher differs from Methodius' creation of the philosophical Thecla and Gregory's treatment of Macrina across only two texts. Monica is characterized not only across a narrative text (the *Confessions*) and a dialogic text but across multiple dialogic texts.

In addition to her role in the *De Beata Vita*, the *De Ordine*, and the *Confessions*, she makes a cameo in the *Contra Academicos* 2.5.

> And when he [Alypius] was trying to say the rest, our mother – for we had now arrived at home – began to push us into lunch, so we had no more time to make conversation.
>
> et cum reliqua dicere tenderet, mater nostra – nam domi iam eramus – ita nos trudere in prandium coepit, ut uerba faciendi locus non esset.

They stop talking *as a result* of Monica's actions, but it is not constructed as her *purpose* to halt the conversation. Her purpose is pro-lunch rather than anti-conversation. Her nonverbal role in the *Contra Academicos* ties her more closely to the world of practicalities (G. Clark 2015, 98–99, 109–10). However, the tables are turned in *De Ordine*, when she is summoned from the discussion to their physical lunch (Aug. *De Ord.* 2.6.18).[53] She is not only the support of the intellectual life led and organized by her son, but can also flip to the other side and be a participant as well.

---

[53] In a similar vein, Augustine in the *De Beata Vita* develops a prevalent metaphor of their conversation as the birthday meal that he is providing to his friends and family (Aug. *De Beat. Vit.* 1.6, 4.36). Then, on the second day, he expands this to say that God is the best host of a truly nourishing intellectual meal (Aug. *De Beat. Vit.* 3.17). Monica participates in this intellectual birthday symposium.

Monica's two lunches show us how Augustine shapes Monica's roles in different ways across texts, and what a flexible character she is in his hands. Another example can be found in two moments when Monica interacts with sacred songs. Early in the *De Ordine* Augustine tells us that Monica had overheard Licentius singing Psalms while in the toilet. She complained to him that the toilet is a wholly inappropriate place to sing such things. In the process, Augustine calls her not only "our mother" (*mater nostra*) but also "a most religious woman" (*religiosissima femina*, Aug. *De Ord.* 1.8.22). Her chastening of Licentius is brought up the next day by Augustine. Having a tête-à-tête with Licentius, he explains how the toilet is *not* an incongruous place to sing for God's help, but rather a genuine cry for salvation which God heard (Aug. *De Ord.* 1.8.23). Here, then, Monica's sensitivities, her literal-mindedness, are seen as incorrectly interpreting a situation, unable to move into metaphorical reality as her son is able to do. Augustine might not only intend the description of her as hyper-religious (*religiosissima femina*) in praise.

The *De Beata Vita* ends with Monica's appropriate singing of the last line of one of Ambrose's new songs, the *Deus Creator Omnium*. Augustine describes her as "waking up to her faith" (*quasi euigilans in fidem suam*) and singing "Refresh your petitioners, O Trinity" (*fove precantes, trinitas*, Aug. *De Beat. Vit.* 4.37). Her melodic response to Augustine's final long monologue is seen as a suitable close to the day's birthday discussions. Although Monica got it wrong in the *De Ordine*, being too careful about the application of sacred song, here she gets it right, finding the suitable hymn for the occasion and rounding off the ending with an elevated contribution.

4.3 Conclusion

We witnessed Thecla's transformation into a philosopher in the first section of this Element, when she was moved into a philosophical dialogue by Methodius from her earlier narrative role as a holy witness in her *Acts*. The suspicion that the change in characterization has much to do with the genre in which Thecla found herself is supported by the evidence of Augustine's characterization of his mother Monica. He explicitly characterizes Monica as a philosopher multiple times in his philosophical dialogues. Yet, when he moves her into a narrative as a supporting character in his *Confessions*, he does not draw explicitly upon the terminology of philosophy.

Augustine presents an education of Monica in the *Confessions*, but it is a moral rather than a literary education. Perhaps even more surprisingly, it is a failed moral education. The wise slave teacher did not succeed in teaching temperance, which was only brought to bear in Monica through the harsh words of another slave. God used those words to teach Monica directly. The direct access that Monica has to truth, which is a recurring trope in both the dialogues and the *Confessions*, comes from her liturgical life, her mode of comprehension that also is closely attuned to the Psalms and the hymns of Ambrose. Likewise, as we discussed in the *De Ordine*, at times Augustine wants to point out that Monica has access to wisdom because of her religious life, while at other times he emphasizes her talent (*ingenium*, Aug. *De Ord.* 2.1.1) and mind suited to philosophy (*tanta mens … aptius verae philosophiae*, Aug. *De Ord.* 2.1.1), tying philosophy more closely to the ability to carry out rational discussion than to apprehension through alternative, liturgical means.

And how does Monica's status as a philosopher relate to the theme of "becoming female"? When Augustine narrates the dropping away of the senses in the mystical ascent at Ostia, Monica's co-journeying ends in the feminization of both. They are equally submissive to the power that conquers them, equally at the end of their ability, equally passive in the face of utter power. The ascent, made now through desire rather than through tools of traditional education, can flip the gendered expectations that were traditional in the metaphor. Augustine brings the feminine into himself,[54] and in that feminine aspect his secular accomplishments are nothing.

5 Conclusion

Genre impinges on how early Christian female philosophers are characterized across different works. Thecla entered into the roll call of philosophers when her legend was moved into a philosophical dialogue. Augustine left behind his concern with characterizing Monica as a philosopher when she exited his dialogues and moved into his *Confessions*. In contrast, Gregory of Nyssa uses just as much philosophical terminology about Macrina in the narrative biography as he does in his dialogue. Yet Macrina's philosophical characterization is done differently when she is in verbal mode or narrative mode. The dialogic Macrina, even if equally characterized as a philosopher as her biographical version, is more learned in secular knowledge – something she is explicitly kept from in the *Life*.

Across their representations, authors most often attribute professional philosophical knowledge to women when they are in verbal mode. The internal narrators in Methodius' *Symposium* assert that Thecla was educated in the liberal arts as well as sacred doctrine – and she shows this with her knowledge

---

[54] We should not forget that another work that Augustine wrote while in Cassiciacum was his *Soliloquy*, where he carried out a conversation with his Reason (*Ratio*), another abstract noun gendered feminine. But this time, it is part of himself rather than an external goal.

of numerology and astronomy. Macrina displays knowledge of astronomy, mechanics, and ethics when she is in a dialogue in a way that seems at odds with her characterization in the *Life of Macrina*.

Secular education is something that is worried over, developed, removed, and talked about for Christian female philosophers. And while the women in this Element were granted participation in some aspects of secular philosophy, other Christians made the nexus of religion, philosophy, and gender more antagonistic. For example, Lactantius, writing his *Divine Institutes* in the early years of the fourth century CE, pits Christian life against philosophy, precisely because of the prerequisites for philosophy's pursuit, among which he names geometry, music, and astronomy. Such onerous requirements make it impossible for whole classes of people to participate in the philosophical life. For instance, he asserts that philosophers have only ever managed to teach one woman (*denique nullas unquam mulieres philosophari docuerunt, praeter unam ex omni memoria Themisten*, Lactantius *Divine Institutes* 3.25).[55] The reason Lactantius gives for this patently false claim is the patently true statement that women, like slaves, are kept too busy by their duties for the necessary education and accompanying leisure required. Lactantius' larger argument is that Christianity, unlike philosophy, makes the good life available to those who are not elite men with the necessary free time.

However, there was another solution to the problem of the time-pressed and overburdened woman. She could be removed from her household and familial duties. Christianity's championing of female asceticism curated a setting in which women's time was freed to pursue topics of the mind. Thecla abandoned her betrothed to follow Paul; Macrina advised her mother to become a philosopher once her children were grown; Monica is described in philosophical terms only when she is an old woman and not living in her own house with all the duties of care that necessitated. Celibacy, and freedom from child-rearing and household management, opened up new spaces of time, and the ascetic life took over much of the discourse around philosophy.

However, Thecla, Macrina, and Monica are not only models of ascetic ideals but also educational ideals, verbal ideals, conversationalist ideals. Philosophy was not only a way of life for some early Christian authors but also a way of speaking. This is one particular way that adding in philosophical dialogues featuring women enriches the story – it shows the care and focus on the female voice. Women were not only used to show that secular knowledge was unnecessary for wisdom. Instead, some authors also wanted to show women using the

---

[55] This is Themista of Lampsacus, who was a student of Epicurus. See D. L. 10.25–26; Cicero *De Finibus* 2.21.68; and Clement of Alexandria *Stromateis* 4.121.4.

extra time freed up by an ascetical life to gain secular knowledge and use it for distinctly Christian philosophical arguments. What I have endeavored to show in this Element is that women in certain early Christian texts participate in a more formalized and secular form of education-led philosophy. The story is messier than certain apologists like Lactantius wished to make out. The life of learning, and not only the life of asceticism and martyrdom, became something that some writers attributed to women. Philosophy could be understood not only as ethical living but in a way that might very well require formal and systematic intellectual training.

When men chose to use the female voice to discuss philosophical issues, they decided, in some important ways, to enter into the psyche of women, to think like the "other" and write like the "other." Wise women become models not only for other women but also for these male writers and their predominantly male audiences. At times, as with Macrina's character in *On the Soul and Resurrection*, the importance of the feminine seems to drop away. But at other times, such as in Methodius' *Symposium* and Augustine's *Confessions*, it seems that men celebrated women *in their femininity* as something to imitate. Men chose to commemorate these women as philosophers, and to script them into conversation. When they did so, they became ideals not only for women to imitate but for men too.

Abbreviations

ATh	*The Acts of Paul and Thecla*
Aug. *Conf.*	Augustine's *Confessions*
Aug. *De Beat. Vit.*	Augustine' s *De Beata Vita*
Aug. *De Ord.*	Augustine's *De Ordine*
D. L.	Diogenes Laertius' *Lives of the Philosophers*
Meth. *Symp.*	Methodius of Olympus' *Symposium*
Meth. *De Lep.*	Methodius of Olympus' *De Lepra*
Greg. Nyss. *Vit. Macr.*	Gregory of Nyssa's *Life of Macrina*
Greg. Nyss. *De Anima*	Gregory of Nyssa's *On the Soul and Resurrection*

References

Addey, Crystal. 2017. "Plato's Women Readers." In *Brill's Companion to the Reception of Plato in Antiquity*, edited by Harold Tarrant, Danielle A. Layne, Dirk Baltzly, and François Renaud, 411–32. Leiden: Brill.

Albrecht, Ruth. 1986. *Das Leben der heiligen Makrina auf den Hintergrund der Thekla-Traditionen: Studien zu den Ursprüngen des weiblichen Mönchtums im 4. Jahrhundert in Kleinasien*. Vol. 38. Forschungen zur Kirchen- und Dogmengeschichte. Göttingen: Vandenhoeck & Ruprecht.

Aspegren, Kerstin. 1995. *The Male Woman: A Feminine Ideal in the Early Church*. Uppsala: Acta Universitatis Upsaliensis.

Barrier, Jeremy W. 2009. *The Acts of Paul and Thecla: A Critical Introduction and Commentary*. Tübingen: Mohr Siebeck.

Boin, Douglas Ryan. 2010. "Late Antique Ostia and a Campaign for Pious Tourism: Epitaphs for Bishop Cyriacus and Monica, Mother of Augustine." *The Journal of Roman Studies* 100 (November): 195–209.

Bowery, Anne-Marie. 2007. "Monica: The Feminine Face of Christ." In *Feminist Interpretations of Augustine*, edited by Judith Chelius Stark, 69–95. University Park, PA: The Pennsylvania State University Press.

Bracht, Katharina. 1999. *Vollkommenheit und Vollendung zur Anthropologie des Methodius von Olympus*. Studien und Texte zu Antike und Christentum / Studies and Texts in Antiquity and Christianity. Tübingen: Mohr Siebeck.

Broux, Yanne, and Mark Depauw. 2015. "The Maternal Line in Greek Identification: Signalling Social Status in Roman Egypt (30 BC–AD 400)." *Historia: Zeitschrift für Alte Geschichte* 64 (4): 467–78.

Burns, Dylan M. 2017. "Astrological Determinism, Free Will, and Desire According to Thecla (St. Methodius, *Symposium* 8.15–16)." In *Women and Knowledge in Early Christianity*, edited by Ulla Tervahauta, Ivan Miroshnikov, Outi Lehtipuu, and Ismo Dunderberg, 206–20. Leiden: Brill.

Burrus, Virginia. 1987. *Chastity as Autonomy: Women in the Stories of the Apocryphal Acts*. Vol. 23. Studies in Women and Religion. Lewiston, NY: Edwin Mellen Press.

2000. *"Begotten, Not Made": Conceiving Manhood in Late Antiquity*. Redwood City, CA: Stanford University Press.

2005. "Is Macrina a Woman? Gregory of Nyssa's *Dialogue on the Soul and Resurrection*." In *The Blackwell Companion to Postmodern Theology*, edited by Graham Ward, 249–64. Oxford: Blackwell.

2007. *The Sex Lives of Saints: An Erotics of Ancient Hagiography*. Divinations: Rereading Late Ancient Religion. Philadelphia: University of Pennsylvania Press.

Candido, Federica. 2017. "The *Symposium* of Methodius: A Witness to the Existence of Circles of Christian Women in Asia Minor? Some Conjectures about an Interpretation That Goes Beyond Literal Fiction." In *Methodius of Olympus: State of the Art and New Perspectives*, edited by Katharina Bracht, 103–24. Berlin: De Gruyter.

Castelli, Elizabeth. 1991. "'I Will Make Mary Male': Pieties of the Body and Gender Transformation of Christian Women in Late Antiquity." In *Body Guards: The Cultural Politics of Gender Ambiguity*, edited by Julia Epstein and Kristina Straub, 29–49. New York: Routledge.

Champion, Michael. 2014. "Grief and Desire, Body and Soul in Gregory of Nyssa's *Life of Saint Macrina*." In *Conjunctions of Mind, Soul and Body from Plato to the Enlightenment*, edited by Danijela Kambraskovic, 99–118. Vol. 15. Studies in the History of Philosophy of Mind. Dordrecht: Springer.

Clark, Elizabeth. 1999. "Rewriting Early Christian History: Augustine's Representation of Monica." In *Portraits of Spiritual Authority: Religious Power in Early Christianity, Byzantium and the Christian Orient*, edited by Jan Willem Drijvers and John W. Watt, 3–23. Leiden: Brill.

Clark, Elizabeth A. 1998. "The Lady Vanishes: Dilemmas of a Feminist Historian after the 'Linguistic Turn.'" *Church History* 67 (1): 1–31.

Clark, Gillian. 2007. "Do Try This at Home: The Domestic Philosopher in Late Antiquity." In *From Rome to Constantinople: Studies in Honour of Averil Cameron*, edited by Hagit Amirav and Bas ter Haar Romeny, 153–72. Leuven: Peeters.

2008. "Can We Talk? Augustine and the Possibility of Dialogue." In *The End of Dialogue in Antiquity*, edited by Simon Goldhill, 117–34. Cambridge: Cambridge University Press.

2015. *Monica: An Ordinary Saint*. Women in Antiquity. Oxford: Oxford University Press.

Clement of Alexandria. 1954 *Christ the Educator*. Translated by Simon P. Wood. Washington D.C.: Catholic University of America Press.

Cloke, Gillian. 1994. *This Female Man of God: Women and Spiritual Power in the Patristic Age 350–450*. London: Routledge.

Connell, Sophia M. 2016. *Aristotle on Female Animals: A Study of the Generation of Animals*. Cambridge Classical Studies. Cambridge: Cambridge University Press. https://doi.org/10.1017/CBO9781316479766.

Conybeare, Catherine. 2006. *The Irrational Augustine.* Oxford: Oxford University Press.

Cooper, Kate. 1996. *The Virgin and the Bride: Idealized Womanhood in Late Antiquity.* Cambridge, MA: Harvard University Press.

Courcelle, Pierre. 1970. "Le personnage de Philosophie dans la littérature latine." *Journal des savants* 4: 209–52.

Daniélou, Jean. 1961. "La notion de confins (μεθόριος) chez Grégoire de Nysse." *Recherches de Science Religieuse* 49 (2): 161–87.

Davies, Stevan L. 1980. *The Revolt of the Widows: The Social World of the Apocryphal Acts.* Carbondale, IL: Southern Illinois University Press.

1986. "Women, Tertullian and the Acts of Paul." *Semeia* 38: 139–43.

Davis, Stephen J. 2002. "Crossed Texts, Crossed Sex: Intertextuality and Gender in Early Christian Legends of Holy Women Disguised as Men." *Journal of Early Christian Studies* 10 (1): 1–36. https://doi.org/10.1353/earl.2002.0003.

2008. *The Cult of Saint Thecla: A Tradition of Women's Piety in Late Antiquity.* Oxford Early Christian Studies. Oxford: Oxford University Press.

2015. "From Women's Piety to Male Devotion: Gender Studies, the 'Acts of Paul and Thecla', and the Evidence of an Arabic Manuscript." *The Harvard Theological Review* 108 (4): 579–93.

DePalma Digeser, Elizabeth. 2017. *A Threat to Public Piety: Christians, Platonists, and the Great Persecution.* Ithaca, NY: Cornell University Press.

Deslauriers, Marguerite. 2012. "Women, Education, and Philosophy." In *A Companion to Women in the Ancient World*, edited by Sharon L. James and Sheila Dillon, 343–53. Oxford: John Wiley & Sons.

2022. *Aristotle on Sexual Difference: Metaphysics, Biology, Politics.* Oxford: Oxford University Press.

Dillon, John. 2004. "Philosophy as a Profession in Late Antiquity." In *Approaching Late Antiquity: The Transformation from Early to Late Empire*, edited by Simon Swain and Mark Edwards, 401–18. Oxford: Oxford University Press.

Dorandi, T. 1989. "Assiotea e Lastenia: due donne all'Accademia." *Atti e Memorie Accademia Toscana 'La Colombaria'* 54: 53–66.

Dutsch, Dorota M. 2020. *Pythagorean Women Philosophers: Between Belief and Suspicion. Pythagorean Women Philosophers.* Oxford Studies in Classical Literature and Gender Theory. Oxford: Oxford University Press.

Evans, Ernest. 1964. *Tertullian's Homily on Baptism. The Text Edited with an Introduction, Translation and Commentary.* London: SPCK.

Eyl, Jennifer. 2013. "Why Thekla Does Not See Paul: Visual Perception and the Displacement of Erōs in the *Acts of Paul and Thekla*." In *The Ancient Novel and the Early Christian and Jewish Narrative: Fictional Intersections*, edited by Judith Perkins and Mariliá Futre Pinheiro, 3–19. Groningen: Barkhuis Publishing.

Fiorenza, Elisabeth Schussler. 1994. *In Memory of Her: A Feminist Theological Reconstruction of Christian Origins*. 10th anniversary edition. New York: The Crossroad Publishing Company.

Frank, Georgia. 2000. "Macrina's Scar: Homeric Allusion and Heroic Identity in Gregory of Nyssa's *Life of Macrina*." *Journal of Early Christian Studies* 8 (4): 511–30.

Goehring, James E. 1981. "A Classical Influence on the Gnostic Sophia Myth." *Vigiliae Christianae* 35 (1): 16–23. https://doi.org/10.2307/1583354.

Hadot, Pierre. 1995. *Philosophy as a Way of Life: Spiritual Exercises from Socrates to Foucault*. Edited by Arnold Davidson. Translated by Michael Chase. Oxford: Blackwell.

Hayes, Leslie K. 2016. "The Acts of Thecla: Introduction, Translation, and Notes." Unpublished Ph.D. dissertation, Claremont Graduate University, California.

Hayne, Léonie. 1994. "Thecla and the Church Fathers." *Vigiliae Christianae* 48 (3): 209–18.

Helleman, Wendy Elgersma. 2009. *The Feminine Personification of Wisdom: A Study of Homer's* Penelope, *Cappadocian* Macrina, *Boethius'* Philosophia, *and Dante's* Beatrice. Lewiston: Edwin Mellen Press.

Hotchkiss, Valerie R. 1996. *Clothes Make the Man: Female Cross Dressing in Medieval Europe*. New York: Routledge.

Johnson, Aaron P. 2013. *Religion and Identity in Porphyry of Tyre: The Limits of Hellenism in Late Antiquity*. Greek Culture in the Roman World. Cambridge: Cambridge University Press. https://doi.org/10.1017/CBO9780511998546.

Kraemer, Ross Shepard. 1992. *Her Share of the Blessings: Women's Religions among Pagans, Jews, and Christians in the Greco-Roman World*. New York: Oxford University Press.

Kraemer, Ross Shepard. 2019. "Thecla." In *The Oxford Handbook of New Testament, Gender, and Sexuality*, edited by Benjamin Dunning, 485–502. Oxford: Oxford University Press.

Krueger, Derek. 2000. "Writing and the Liturgy of Memory in Gregory of Nyssa's *Life of Macrina*." *Journal of Early Christian Studies* 8 (4): 483–510.

Lauwers, Jeroen. 2013. "Systems of Sophistry and Philosophy: The Case of the Second Sophistic." *Harvard Studies in Classical Philology* 107: 331–63.

LaValle Norman, Dawn. 2019a. "Becoming Female: Marrowy Semen and the Formative Mother in Methodius of Olympus's *Symposium*." *Journal of Early Christian Studies* 27 (2): 185–209. https://doi.org/10.1353/earl.2019 .0018.

2019b. *The Aesthetics of Hope in Late Greek Imperial Literature: Methodius of Olympus'* Symposium *and the Crisis of the Third Century*. Greek Culture in the Roman World. Cambridge: Cambridge University Press.

2023. "Female Characters as Modes of Knowing in Late Imperial Dialogues: The Body, Desire, and the Intellectual Life." In *The Intellectual World of Late Antique Christianity: Reshaping Classical Traditions*, edited by Lewis Ayres, Michael Champion, and Matthew Crawford. Cambridge: Cambridge University Press.

Leitao, David D. 2012. *The Pregnant Male As Myth and Metaphor in Classical Greek Literature*. Cambridge: Cambridge University Press.

Leyerle, Blake. 1995. "Clement of Alexandria on the Importance of Table Etiquette." *Journal of Early Christian Studies* 3 (2): 123–41. https://doi .org/10.1353/earl.0.0041.

Ludlow, Morwenna. 2009. "Science and Theology in Gregory of Nyssa's *De Anima et Resurrectione*: Astronomy and Automata." *The Journal of Theological Studies* 60 (2): 467–89.

MacDonald, Dennis Ronald. 1983. *The Legend and the Apostle, The Battle for Paul in Story and Canon*. Philadelphia: Westminster Press.

Maciver, Calum. 2007. "Returning to the Mountain of *Arete*: Reading Ecphrasis, Constructing Ethics in Quintus Smyrnaeus' *Posthomerica*." In *Quintus Smyrnaeus: Transforming Homer in Second Sophistic Epic*, edited by Manuel Baumbach and Silvio Bär, 259–84. Berlin: De Gruyter.

Malingrey, Anne-Marie. 1961. *Philosophia: étude d'un groupe de mots dans la littérature grecque, des Présocratiques au IVe siècle apres J.C.* Paris: C. Klincksieck.

Maraval, Pierre, trans. 1971. *Vie de Sainte Macrine. Grégoire de Nysse*. Sources chrétiennes no. 178. Paris: Editions du Cerf.

Marx, Heidi. 2021. *Sosipatra of Pergamum: Philosopher and Oracle*. Women in Antiquity. Oxford: Oxford University Press.

McGuckin, John Anthony. 2001. *St. Gregory of Nazianzus: An Intellectual Biography*. Crestwood, NY: St Vladimir's Seminary Press.

Methodius of Olympus. 2015. "On the Distinction Between Foods (De Cibis)." Translated by Ralph Cleminson. www.roger-pearse.com.

Miles, Margaret. 1989. *Carnal Knowing: Female Nakedness and Religious Meaning in the Christian West*. Eugene, OR: Wipf and Stock Publishers.

Muehlberger, Ellen. 2015. "Simeon and Other Women in Theodoret's Religious History: Gender in the Representation of Late Ancient Christian Asceticism." *Journal of Early Christian Studies* 23 (4): 583–606. https://doi.org/10.1353/earl.2015.0050.

Musurillo, Herbert, ed. 1963. *Méthode d'Olympe. Le Banquet*. Translated by Victor-Henry Debidour. Vol. 95. Sources Chrétiennes. Paris: Les Éditions du Cerf.

O'Donnell, James. 1992. *Augustine's* Confessions. *III. Commentary on Books 8–13. Indexes*. Oxford: Clarendon Press.

O'Meara, Dominic J. 1990. *Pythagoras Revived: Mathematics and Philosophy in Late Antiquity*. Oxford: Clarendon Press.

Patterson, L. G. 1997. *Methodius of Olympus: Divine Sovereignty, Human Freedom, and Life in Christ*. Washington, D.C.: Catholic University of America Press.

Pellò, Caterina. 2022. *Pythagorean Women*. Cambridge Elements: Women in the History of Philosophy. Cambridge: Cambridge University Press.

Plato. 1997. *Phaedo*. Translated by G. M. A. Grube. In *Plato: Complete Works*, edited by John M. Cooper, 49–100. Indianapolis: Hackett Publishing Company.

Ptolemy. 1998. *Ptolemy's Almagest*. Princeton, NJ: Princeton University Press.

Ramelli, Ilaria. 2020. "Religion and Science in Gregory of Nyssa: The Unity of the Creative and Scientific Logos." *Marburg Journal of Religion* 22 (2): 1–16.

Rordorf, Willy. 1986. "Tradition and Composition in the Acts of Thecla: The State of the Question." *Semeia* 38: 43–52.

Rosen, Ralph Mark, and Ineke Sluiter, eds. 2003. *Andreia: Studies in Manliness and Courage in Classical Antiquity*. Mnemosyne, Bibliotheca Classica Batava. Supplementum, 238. Leiden: Brill.

Sehorn, John. 2015. "Monica as Synecdoche for the Pilgrim Church in the *Confessiones*." *Augustinian Studies* 46 (2): 225–48. https://doi.org/10.5840/augstudies2015111115.

Shaw, Brent D. 1987. "The Age of Roman Girls at Marriage: Some Reconsiderations." *The Journal of Roman Studies* 77: 30–46. https://doi.org/10.2307/300573.

Silvas, Anna M. 2008. *Macrina the Younger: Philosopher of God*. Turnhout: Brepols Publishers.

Smith, David E. 2002. *The Canonical Function of Acts: A Comparative Analysis*. Collegeville, MN: Liturgical Press.

Smith, J. Warren. 2004. *Passion and Paradise: Human and Divine Emotion in the Thought of Gregory of Nyssa*. New York: Herder.

Stanton, G. R. 1973. "Sophists and Philosophers: Problems of Classification." *The American Journal of Philology* 94 (4): 350–64. https://doi.org/10.2307/293614.

Tervahauta, Ulla, Ivan Miroshnikov, Outi Lehtipuu, and Ismo Dunderberg, eds. 2017. *Women and Knowledge in Early Christianity*. Leiden: Brill.

Upson-Saia, Kristi. 2011. *Early Christian Dress: Gender, Virtue, and Authority*. New York: Routledge.

Urbano, Arthur P. 2013. *The Philosophical Life: Biography and the Crafting of Intellectual Identity in Late Antiquity*. Washington D.C.: Catholic University of America Press.

Vaught, Carl G. 2004. *Encounters with God in Augustine's Confessions Books VII–IX*. Albany, NY: State University of New York Press.

Whalin, Douglas. 2021. "Mountains and the Holy in Late Antiquity." In *Mountain Dialogues from Antiquity to Modernity*, edited by Dawn Hollis and Jason König, 89–107. London: Bloomsbury.

Wilson-Kaster, Patricia. 1979. "Macrina: Virgin and Teacher." *Andrews University Seminary Studies* 17 (1): 105–17.

Wycherley, R. E. 1959. "The Garden of Epicurus." *Phoenix* 13 (2): 73–77.

Acknowledgments

I would like to thank the following for their helpful feedbacks on earlier drafts of this work: Crystal Addey, Michael Champion, Matthew Crawford, Sarah Gador-Whyte, Erika Kidd, Veronica Roberts, John Sehorn, and Jonathan Zecher.

The research for this Element was funded by the Australian Government through the Australian Research Council project number DE220100854.

Cambridge Elements ☰

Women in the History of Philosophy

Jacqueline Broad
Monash University

Jacqueline Broad is Associate Professor of Philosophy at Monash University, Australia. Her area of expertise is early modern philosophy, with a special focus on seventeenth and eighteenth-century women philosophers. She is the author of *Women Philosophers of the Seventeenth Century* (CUP, 2002), *A History of Women's Political Thought in Europe, 1400–1700* (with Karen Green; CUP, 2009), and *The Philosophy of Mary Astell: An Early Modern Theory of Virtue* (OUP, 2015).

Advisory Board

About the Series

In this Cambridge Elements series, distinguished authors provide concise and structured introductions to a comprehensive range of prominent and lesser-known figures in the history of women's philosophical endeavour, from ancient times to the present day.

Cambridge Elements ≡

Women in the History of Philosophy

Elements in the Series

A full series listing is available at: www.cambridge.org/EWHP

Printed in the United States
by Baker & Taylor Publisher Services